Giovanni Maio

Understanding the Patient

VERLAG KARL ALBER

Becoming ill can plunge people into an existential crisis. Modern medicine reacts to this by applying methods of natural science and by using state-of-the-art technology, but it often leaves the person, who is suffering this crisis, alone. Giovanni Maio draws attention to the one-sidedness of medical treatment which is oriented towards natural science and develops an ethical approach to medicine based on the power of understanding and care. He provides examples of this that are taken from medical practice. In a »small phenomenology of illness« he illustrates how, in the case of chronic pain, cancer, dementia or in the final stages of a terminally ill patient's life, the curative power of understanding can be brought to bear on the field of medicine.

The Author:

Giovanni Maio, Philosopher and Medic, is Professor of Medical Ethics at the Albert-Ludwigs University of Freiburg and Director of the Institute of Medical Ethics and History of Medicine.

Giovanni Maio

Understanding the Patient

An Ethical Approach to Medical Care

Translated into English
by David Carus

Verlag Karl Alber Freiburg / München

Originally published in German as »Den kranken Menschen verstehen. Für eine Medizin der Zuwendung«

MIX
Papier aus verantwortungsvollen Quellen
FSC® C083411

English first edition

www.verlag-alber.de

Cover photo: © Evelyn Dilworth – Fotolia
Typesetting: SatzWeise GmbH, Trier
Printed and bound by: CPI books GmbH, Leck

Printed in Germany

ISBN 978-3-495-48898-0

Contents

Preface

This book has grown out of years of work looking at misguided developments in modern medical practice, a theme I have addressed in several other books. At some point, I felt the need to go beyond critical examination and set out to explore what is important to me in a positive way. All around me, I see both young and experienced doctors who, in spite of adverse circumstances, are happy to have chosen their particular occupation because they feel that as doctors they have the opportunity to provide something meaningful and purposeful to others every day. There are so many doctors who, in striving to help others, expose themselves each day to the suffering of people who are ill and who, in order to solve those people's problems, again and again reach out for solutions, so that they, the others, feel better. In an age when the public is increasingly losing trust in medical practice, mainly owing to its widespread economisation, it is important to make clear that this practice today and every day is still a social practice of care aimed at people in need of help. However, it must be pointed out that those practising it are doing so not because of the structures in place, but in spite of the structures, which in terms of the interpersonal character of medical practice are now under more threat than ever before. It seemed important to me to point out that the type of medical treatment that people who are ill desire still exists, but that medical practice is increasingly on the defensive because it is judged on criteria that have virtually nothing to do with care, understanding and support.

What I am hoping to achieve with this book is, on the one

hand, to offer patients reassurance, and on the other hand, to embolden doctors, psychotherapists, caregivers, midwives, physiotherapists, and all those who continually offer their services to people in inpatient and outpatient facilities not to allow economisation to strip them of their inner values. I hope and trust I can reawaken the dormant impulse in the vast majority of doctors, as human beings, to devote themselves to people who are suffering. After the books I have written in recent years, where I criticised medical practice, this book is intended as a book of encouragement. After all, the biggest asset we have is that inherent impulse, that great intrinsic motivation of the health care professions, which is, however, gradually being undermined by the system. This undermining must be stopped and this can only succeed by raising awareness of how worthwhile and valuable this inner motivation to be there for others actually is. For a human being is not simply a *homo oeconomicus*, but instead is fundamentally oriented towards other people. We learn almost everything that is to be learned from other people and we can make nothing of ourselves on our own. The possibility of giving others the feeling that they are not alone in their distress, the possibility that every person has the chance to give back in many ways what which we have received from others, is exactly what medical practice can offer.

Acknowledgments

I too am aware that I owe everything to others. This is not the place to thank all those who have made it possible for me to do what I am able to do today, but it is the place to thank those who have made it possible to bring about this book, a book that has been occupying my thoughts for the last few years. First and foremost, I would like to thank my esteemed publisher Herder! They were interested in my idea from the beginning, encouraged me in my work, and did their utmost to support me. It was the excellent collaboration with this publisher that intensified my pleasure in writing, and for this I would like to offer my sincere thanks, above all to Dr. German Neundorfer for his careful editing, all his constructive and instructive advice and for his dedicated and committed companionship during the long creative phase. I would also like to offer my particular thanks to Dr. Tobias Winstel who, as publishing director, made a number of suggestions and who has consistently encouraged me to retain the exact style which we had initially and quickly agreed upon. Last but not least, I would like to thank Mr Manuel Herder himself, whose appreciative support means a lot to me.

I wish to offer my sincere thanks to Dr. Cathrin Nielsen. She has assisted me in almost all my books, knows my thoughts better than almost anyone else and without her initial meticulous revision of my manuscripts the book would not have assumed its present form. I want to express my sincere thanks for all the time she has devoted to me and for all her sensitivity in truly engaging with my thoughts.

It is also of great importance to me to thank Dr. Raphael

Rauh who proofread the manuscript with unsurpassable diligence and erudition; working with him was, as always, a great pleasure.

Finally, I would like to thank all the doctors, all the psychotherapists and all the patients who write to me every day and who I have the pleasure to meet on my lecture tours. Their interests, their ideas, their worries and their support have been incorporated into the following pages. None of our thoughts arise simply from ourselves alone – ultimately, it is dialogue with others that spurs us on towards new ideas. I hope the ideas in this book benefit those for whom they have been developed: people who are ill.

Freiburg, July 2015

I. Modern Medical Practice: when understanding the patient becomes a secondary issue

> »No method can replace personal warmth, tolerance and a positive mindset towards people.«
>
> *Ruth C. Cohn*

In everyday work at the clinic we often find that those who are seriously ill thank doctors effusively when they are discharged from the clinic and are full of praise for the treatment they have received from the doctors, nurses and carers. On closer inspection, we come to realise that this praise is less about the success of the actual treatment than the fact that these patients were able to voice their concerns and fears. They are grateful that they were able to speak about themselves and their worries. It is simply the feeling of being understood that brings about this underlying sentiment of thankfulness. Even though many people still feel they can find a friendly ear at their doctor's surgery it is certainly not self-evident in today's world. After all, in the manner it is set up, with its structural conditions and indeed in its very credo, modern medical practice is far more focused on function than understanding. There are several reasons for this.

Medical practice as an industrial enterprise?

Modern medical practice relies on science, technology and repair, as if illness were merely a defect to be rectified. In line with this concept of medicine, all its energy is directed towards »doing«, towards the application of procedures. We fail to recognise that someone who is ill is often helped more through understanding and a proper relationship with his or her doctor. The fact that modern medical practice is in danger of losing sight of the healing power of understanding is due to the fact that we are living in an era where numbers, measurement, demonstration and calculation have gained a new and very powerful meaning. Although for 150 years medical practice has been viewed predominantly as an applied natural science – and to a certain extent measurement is a part of this tradition – the prevailing orientation is now towards natural science, not least because this comes hand in hand with a momentous and far-reaching shift towards economics. Economics and natural science are so strongly interconnected that dominance of these two paradigms has fundamentally changed the entire field of medical practice. These changes have occurred almost entirely unnoticed, as they are of an inherent nature. They concern our fundamental understanding of medical practice, its inner identity, possibly even more so than its external procedures. Performing, measuring, examining, demonstrating – these are all required today and not simply where processes take place, as is the case in industry, but rather where the sole concern is the human being. The treatment of people who are ill is increasingly being oriented towards the theoretical guidelines of industrial production. This has been the *de facto* gateway to a re-evaluation of values in medical practice. For this reason, it is important to think carefully about the difference between the production of objects and the treatment of human beings. Why is medical practice not a process of production? Why are industrial considerations being imposed upon the field of medical practice so unsatisfactory and damaging?

Good medical practice seeks singular solutions

If medical work is to be a process of production, this means it has to be reduced to nothing more than an aggregate of implementations. But not all of what the doctor actually does is contained in the procedure itself. There is a synthesis prior to the procedure, and prior to the synthesis there is a thought process involved in assimilating information from different fields – anamnesis, diagnostics or consideration of the circumstances. Thus, focusing on the procedure leads to a devaluation of the doctor's real medical work and accomplishment, which is contained in the reflective consideration more than in the action itself. When we occasionally speak of »excessive provision« in medical practice, we also have to be aware that the doctors' work is incorrectly being reduced to documentary procedures in the continuing push towards economisation. The process that took place beforehand – the careful approach to diagnosis, the many informal discussions, the invaluable process of reflection – all of this is not taken into consideration. But what would the medical procedure be without all of these preceding actions? The more we evaluate doctors solely on the basis of the number of procedures they have completed and on the parameters that can be assessed, then the more they will forget bit by bit that they in fact perform a lot more than is documented. If this qualitative »more« is not acknowledged, there is a risk that they will become susceptible to the demands of quantity, i.e. to what is quantifiable. But I believe they need not take refuge in the purely quantifiable, instead they should stand up and stoutly defend their competence. The core competence of a doctor lies in skilfully dealing with complexity, in the mastery of insecurity, in the professional handling of incalculables, and ultimately by virtue of these qualifications, in the careful exploration of what is best for the individual patient. The consideration of all these aspects represents the doctor's accomplishments and proficiency, and shows that for a doctor to be a good doctor he or she has to solve problems every day and conceive of something new every day to do justice to the particular individual patient.

Good medical practice demands sensitivity

Against this background, it is possible to reflect more carefully on the difference between production and what medicine accomplishes. Doctors effectuate something through their treatment, but what they in fact effectuate differs from the production process, insofar as they do not create their own product but instead intervene in something which is already there. They intervene in a body, not to produce something new, but to support something which already exists or to change something in such a way as to return the whole body to a balanced state. The doctor intervenes in something living and a good doctor knows full well that if the living body does not contribute its own share to the treatment, all therapeutic effort is in vain. Thus, a doctor intervenes in order to support what already exists and this support all too quickly becomes too much or too little. If what they were doing was a simple process of production, they would only need to look at the diagram and follow the instruction manual. By contrast, in therapeutic practices a manual cannot be followed – it requires reflection, passing judgement through shared dialogue, and sensitivity for the problem at hand.

An organism is complex and the intervention in a living organism infinitely more intricate than the production of an object. Whilst perfect design and standardisation are crucial in the production of something, the most essential element in human therapy is finding the right balance, the balance suitable for a particular patient, to his or her individual findings and history. Ultimately, the value of the treatment does not therefore lie in a perfect formula (as with production), but instead in the cautious examination of what is best for the patient. Circumspection is thus the central aspect in the treatment of those who are ill. The fact that it is precisely this value that is being delegitimised today and that absolutely no meaning is being attributed to it is based on the fundamentally incorrect perception of medical practice as a process of production. It is only against the backdrop of this type of misguided thought that we can understand why in medicine today it there is the expectation to set incorrect incentives and introduce systems of control that are necessarily reductionist.

Reflection and Synthesis

It is this focus on pure performance – which is politically motivated and based on control systems – that leads to too much emphasis on completion and action in modern medical practice. If we implicitly assume that the essence of medical practice can be expressed in measurable data, then this data will continually be developed further without anyone noticing that there has not been any accompanying improvement in quality. Yet the actual quality of a doctor's action is not visible or measurable, but rather is an invisible and immeasurable reflective process. A fundamental problem with this emphasis on action, which can often be seen in modern medical practice, can be explained by the undeniable fact that a great part of medical care is ignored because of the control imperative being imposed upon it, an imperative which has been »borrowed« from industry.

Based on this incorrect line of thought, it is then implied that doctors' medical decisions – as long as they simply stick to the correct process – will always be clearly deducible and algorithmically classifiable. However, medical practice does not function in this way. Not only does the decision about what is to be done ultimately rest with the patient, but it also fails to take account of what medicine is. Situations in medical practice are seldom as clear cut as theory would suggest; in the vast majority of cases there is uncertainty and situations which deal with probabilities, not absolute certainties. Precisely *because* situations always leave an element of uncertainty, a doctor needs to be able to apply discretion in order to suit a decision to a particular situation. The doctor needs freedom of choice in order to be able to make the right assessment; an assessment which is primarily oriented towards the patient from the outset and not set to comply with guidelines, prescribed algorithms or documentary requirements. Today this margin of discretion has been taken away from doctors because the system has not understood what medical care truly is.

Experience and Judgment

It is important to clarify again what medical treatment actually means. Treatment does not mean action *per se*, but rather it concerns making decisions based on what is appropriate for patients and for the particular situation. To be able to do that requires formal expertise; that is, everything that is learnt at university and what is then condensed into guidelines. But the type of practical situation doctors are confronted with is always a unique and distinctive situation, one which is not described in such detail in any textbook and which is not found in any guidelines. This cannot be reduced and simplified owing to the diversity of people and situations. A doctor is, therefore, always confronted with a situation, which, in comparison to his or her expertise is always more complex; it is more complex than formalised knowledge and again and again represents a very particular situation. Doctors must not only possess expertise, they must also know how to deal with each new situation which may arise. Formal expertise alone is not enough to infer what specifically needs to be done; practical judgment is required in order to make the leap from general knowledge to a specific action. This is a skill which goes beyond mere knowledge and represents the real quality of medical care. Immanuel Kant defined judgment as »the talent for selecting what is exactly appropriate in a given case«, as the ability »to find the point about the matter« (*Anthropology from a Pragmatic Point of View,* tr. Robert B. Louden, Cambridge 2006, 123).

The more formalised the guidelines, the more a doctor's ability is jeopardised to make a particular decision suited to the patient. The control which is imposed upon them is demotivating because it implicitly suggests that doctors do not know how to decide for themselves and therefore have to be backed up by formal models. However, these models are already too abstract to be suitable for individual patients. The art of medical practice is defined by the ability to deviate reflectively from a static model and the more doctors are tested on whether they comply with the models, the more they feel patronised. Excellence in medical therapy is not the result of a direct transfer of abstract schemata, but rather results from individual decision making processes based on years of experience. Instructions and guidelines can be guiding principles for this, but they can never take away a doctor's personal decision. They are a support and not the bottom line. Essentially, they are a form of support needed at the start of the job, but which becomes less and less relevant the more experienced the doctor becomes. A person who is highly experienced and who can manage perfectly well will in fact find such support more of a hindrance than an aid. Formalisations always go hand in hand with simplifications, but the art of treatment does not in any way consist in making things simple. Rather it envisages the complexity as well as being able to make the correct decision in the face of uncertainty and mere probabilities, that is to say, a specific situation which can never be completely broken down.

Formalisation assumes clear »cases« and situations, but absolute clarity is seldom found in real practice. We need the medical profession precisely because decisions are not simply made based on facts and because facts alone do not speak for themselves. It is necessary to interpret them and explain them to the patient in such a way that they can be transformed into the patient's long-term interests. This decision might lead to a medical procedure or the decision to conduct further diagnostic tests, but it might also entail the realisation that it would be better to wait or that any further diagnostic tests would only lead to unnecessary risks and might lead to false positives. Whether a medical procedure is unnecessary or not results from direct conversation, from synthesis, from the competence of the doctor and cannot be deduced from formal models. The medical profession exists to bridge the gap between general knowledge and the unique situation of the patient. The judgment necessary to do that cannot be replaced by any treatment scheme, and all the controls which are imposed upon doctors go hand in hand with a disdain for this capacity of judgment and presuppose a conception of medical practice which on closer reflection is untenable. The impression given is that in reality there are only typical cases and no unusual situations, but precisely the opposite is true. Ignoring special unusual situations is a dangerous feature of a business-oriented medical world based on economisation. It is important for doctors to address the indispensability of particularity and to remain aware of it in defiance of these false control systems.

Good Medical Practice: between the art of action and the art of understanding

For all these reasons, medical practice is not about the implementation of a predetermined production process, but instead concerns continually reassessing the particular situation of an ill person, which in turn demands a singular decision. Such a decision is, in the most successful cases, the result of bringing together external expertise and internal knowledge which is the product of the doctor's experience and the actual situation the individual patient is in. This is the real art of medical treatment; an assimilating and unavoidably creative process which cannot be fully predetermined. Instead it must be addressed at a particular moment. What is required for this particular moment is experience, patience and a willingness to communicate. These are all values that are being reduced and neglected today, but are precisely the one which need to be re-evaluated and enhanced. The more these values are ignored and medical practice is simply considered a production process, the more the emphasis on completion will be promoted, activity rewarded, listening penalised, time for intervention calculated, consultation time overlooked, increase in patient-flow given prized status, and caution and care viewed as something which only hinders the smooth running of the business.

For this reason, it is important to bear in mind that, ultimately, medical practice constitutes a combination of calculating and understanding, an alliance between the art of doing and the art of understanding, or the art of speaking. In light of this, in this book I will outline a vision of medicine in which its role is not regarded as something disconnected from human existence, as something which only intervenes in life from outside, if or when the »need for repair« arises. On the contrary, I view medical practice as the answer to the particular hardships of human existence, and for this answer understanding the patient is not a secondary issue, but rather the issue itself. The French phenomenologist Michel Henry expresses it in this way: »Medicine has never been a science in the true sense, not because it lacks rigour. Although it is based on the hard sciences such as biology, chemistry etc., it nevertheless remains »humanistic« in principle. What is meant by this is that all relevant objective knowledge is viewed from the perspective of someone who sees beyond the x-ray of an injury or tumour, i. e. beyond the objective physical body, someone who sees what the consequences are for that felt body, for that self which is alive and suffering, in short for someone who is ill. Without constant reference to this transcendental suffering – which, after all, constitutes human reality – medicine remains incomprehensible.«[1]

With my book, I would like to make it clear that the treatment of sick people is not achieved through impersonal adherence to formal norms, but rather can only be successful when action is embedded in authentic human relationships. In an age of an unhealthy alliance between economy and science, it seems important to me to advocate and call for a new fundamental orientation in medicine. I would like to outline this new point of orientation in the following chapters, alternating between a theoretical framework and a concrete practical phenomenology of the world in which people who are ill live. I will begin with four core challenges faced in modern medicine which I have chosen by way of example for many others cases: pain, cancer, dementia and dying. This choice drives at the very heart of the role of medicine: looking after people who are suffering from symptoms and illnesses

---

[1] Michel Henry, *Inkarnation. Eine Philosophie des Fleisches. Aus dem Französischen von Rolf Kühn.* (Freiburg/Munich: Verlag Karl Alber 2002), p. 350.

that cannot simply be eradicated through a specific course of treatment. It was important to me to focus on chronic, even incurable illnesses, as medicine must take responsibility for these people. After all, they are the ones who are in danger of being forgotten in a medical practice based on economisation.

II.
A small phenomenology of being ill: Real life examples

1. Chronic Pain: Towards a culture of support

> »If there is one lesson to be learned from all of this, it is that nothing can be gained from pain, there is nothing that can be done with pain, yet that one cannot simply leave it be.«
>
> *Christian Grüny*

How we deal with chronic pain tells us a lot about the present imbalance in modern medical practice and about the society in which we live. There are, at present, two different trends. One aims to depict pain as something which is essentially surmountable and preventable. The credo here is: »Pain is unnecessary«. The other presents pain as a purely cognitive phenomenon and places the onus on the individual to have the right attitude and put pain in its place. Thus, patients are left alone to deal with their pain, since they are themselves at fault if they are unsuccessful in adopting the right attitude. Both trends are intrinsically problematic and do not do justice to the phenomenon of pain. This chapter will explain more clearly why this is the case.

Pain as a link between sensory perception and emotion

The central feature of pain is that, from the very beginning, it contains two aspects which cannot be treated as separate issues. On the one hand, pain is a sensory perception. On the other hand it is inextricably linked with an emotion. Pain cannot be discussed without addressing it as an adversary, as something which affects me, moves me and oppresses me. Pain provokes an emotion and immediately gives rise to the desire to rid oneself of it. Pain makes you cry out, people cannot be indifferent to it.

In this respect, pain is not something which can be avoided in a completely detached and matter-of-fact way. Thus, when we are dealing with patients who have chronic pain, we should not tell them that they must learn to live with, or even befriend, their pain. Even considered phenomenologically, I do not think it is possible to regard pain as a friend since the impulse to negate it is inevitably embedded in the experience of pain. In order to help patients with constant pain, we have to recognise that pain is and remains an adversary.

The Totalisation of Adverse Experience

What makes pain dramatic is its tyrannical manifestation. It breaks into your world and spreads itself out, often without advanced notice. From the moment of its arrival it takes over everything. It gives us no leeway; it radically imposes itself on a person and, as Christian Grüny has described it, allows that person no chance to withdraw from it.[1] In this respect, pain is a tyrant. It tyrannises life because it allows no thoughts other than thoughts about itself. This means that pain inevitably interrupts everything we have previously done and which we have previously wanted to do. It does

[1] Christian Grüny, *Zerstörte Erfahrung. Eine Phänomenologie des Schmerzes* (Würzburg: Königshausen & Neumann, 2004), p. 32 ff.

not care who we are, what we want or how we lead our lives. It is suddenly there, tears our life apart and takes everything with it. In so doing, pain results in nothing less than the complete imprisonment of a person. We are captured in the very moment when pain strikes. It makes communication with the outside world impossible, it curtails everyday activities, allows no thoughts of any kind of future and reduces one's being to a being-in-pain,[2] to a being which knows and can relate to nothing more than its pain. Pain, with its tyrannically prescribed breakdown in connections to the outside world, knocks a person out of his unconcern, and makes them forget that life can also be carefree. It makes the moment something exorbitant, something which invokes an absolute revolt. The revolt against pain is so loud that nothing else can be of equal importance to it. Thus, pain brings about a total interruption of life.

Moreover, pain makes a person feel something which he or she can barely endure, namely being someone who does not do something, but rather to whom something is done. Pain is arguably the most dramatic and totalising adverse experience a person can have.[3] It negates the subject and does not ask who we are. By questioning the subject in such a radical way, pain is experienced as a huge threat – a threat to our freedom, a threat to our own self and a threat to all future.[4] People feel at the mercy of pain because they realise it is impossible to find refuge from it. Feeling at the mercy of pain represents a provocation: it cancels out what is naturally important to a person; to be the designer of one's own world. At the moment of acute pain we feel completely powerless,

---

[2] Ibid., p. 37 f.

[3] Burkhard Liebsch, »Außer sich – Zum fragwürdigen ›Vorrecht des Schmerzes‹«. In: *Schmerz als Grenzerfahrung*, ed. by R.-M. E. Jacobi und B. Marx. (Leipzig: Evangelische Verlagsanstalt, 2011), pp. 189–213.

[4] Grüny, *Zerstörte Erfahrung*, p. 172 f.

for we are so much in the grip of pain that we have no other alternative than to »painfully« recognise this passive moment of life.

Pain as an isolating factor

Pain and loneliness are closely interlinked in two ways. Initially pain is something which can only be felt alone. Ultimately, despite all efforts, it is not really communicable. It is something which is necessarily experienced alone, and although understood by others, cannot be felt by them. Pain evades communicability in a way which suffering does not. We can try to explain suffering, we can give reasons for it and rationalise it. Pain, on the other hand, is so basic that it is difficult to express in words. We can paraphrase it, but we cannot understand it in this way. Experiencing pain makes a person feel lonely simply by the fact that one cannot say much about it. Pain can even cause some patients to lose their ability to speak. Pain makes a person speechless and this inability to speak is in stark contrast to the potency which it evokes. However, it is not simply the incommunicability of pain which leads to the phenomenon of isolation. It is much more its totalising characteristic which virtually compels people to shut themselves off from the world.[5] Pain entices patients to withdraw, because patients with chronic pain eventually give up wanting to justify themselves and discuss it with other people; chronic pain overrides the normality of their being and does not allow them to lead a normal life like »other people«. Patients suffering from pain must often live apart from the normal rhythm of other people's lives. They

[5] Ibid., p. 36f.

thus experience every day as alien and as different from other people. They are forced to devise a daily rhythm in which they can live with their pain, beyond the rules which are applicable to everyone else. Patients with chronic pain cannot, therefore, seamlessly integrate into the expectations of a society which is geared towards functioning. In fact, they feel dysfunctional, because their way of life is strikingly different. In this way, chronic pain has an isolating effect because it radically invalidates the efficiency and performance categories of a competitive society. Hence, patients suffering from pain are denied the opportunity to participate in social processes, which leads to social exclusion ranging from a threat of losing their job to economic marginalisation, casualisation and exclusion.

Along with this isolation, another characteristic of chronic pain is its questioning nature. Pain calls everything into question. It calls the future into question. What is the way forward with this pain? How long can I put up with it? Moreover, what is the point in having all this pain? Why me? Why can't I live like everyone else? Why can't I go back to how things were before this pain started? Chronic pain makes us wonder and despair about the point of it all. It makes us despair because it preys on our minds. It eats away at our personality and changes it. It eats away at the smoothness of performance and above all eats away at the feeling of worth and our feeling of self-esteem. Pain imparts a feeling of worthlessness to the person because, occasioned by the pain itself, he cannot apparently fulfil the criteria which appear necessary for a successful life. People lose their feeling of worth because they drop out of the system and because no new system that accepts them emerges in its place.

Subjective experience in a medical world of objectivisation

All phenomena of pain, which have already been described by numerous scholars with slightly different emphases (Buytendijk, von Weizsäcker, Grüny[6]), demonstrate that pain presents an extreme challenge for people. Pain inevitably gives rise to the questions: How can we cope with pain? How can we manage it? How do we escape from it? First and foremost, pain is linked to a cause. A person who has pain always thinks that there is »something« which causes this pain, »something« which breaks in, infiltrates, and tears him or her apart. Understandably, we would like to capture this something and thus the search for an objectifiable cause is the very first access to the pain.[7] The search for the cause of the pain is without doubt necessary and cannot be bypassed. However, what should actually be seen as a *first* step, becomes the only step – becomes a lifelong path for many people.

It is important to overcome this necessary first step if we are to avoid being shackled by it. We wish we had access to the world in such a way that we had an objective answer at the ready for all phenomena, but the world simply is not as we would like it to be. In most cases, an objective cause for the pain cannot be located and it is then necessary to direct one's energy not to the pain, but to other objectives. Of course, it is entirely understandable that in the first instance we prefer to

[6] Frederic J. J. Buytendijk, *Über den Schmerz* (Bern: Huber, 1948); Christian Grüny, *Zerstörte Erfahrung*. C.f. Viktor von Weizsäcker, »Die Schmerzen (1926)«, in *Viktor von Weizsäcker. Collected Works* (Vol.5 ed. by P. Achilles, D. Janz, M. Schrenk and C. F. von Weizsäcker (Frankfurt am Main: Suhrkamp, 1986), pp. 27–47.
[7] Peter Henningsen, »Schmerz und Leiden«, in *Die Schmerzen*, ed. by M. Schiltenwolf and W. Herzog (Würzburg: Königshausen & Neumann, 2011), pp. 161–170, here p. 164 f.

determine the cause since as soon as we have identified an objectifiable reason for the pain, patients suffering the pain feel relieved. They finally feel a sense of legitimacy in experiencing the pain. Constantly have to face an atmosphere of »delegitimation« has become a fundamental problem for patients experiencing pain. That is to say, patients fear that someone could insinuate that their pain is not legitimate because of a missing »cause«; that they are just imagining it or even simulating it. These are the specific fears of a mechanistically oriented society that wishes to »see« objective explanations for all phenomena. In a world geared towards science and technology, it is difficult for some people to understand the idea that pain could be a sensation and experience that results from a complex constellation of our life in its physical, psychological and social forms.

A chronic pain patient as a counterexample to an entrepreneurial self

A world which is structurally biased towards mechanisms gives rise to myths that make life difficult to live, particularly for patients with chronic pain. The most aggravating myth of our time is the myth of control. We tacitly assume that pain is something which can, in principle, be suppressed and is essentially a kind of reparable defect. This can be traced back to ideas of practicality in a society unilaterally oriented towards science and technology.[8] However, this belief in practicality has culminated in today's economist view of humanity. We assume that each person is an entrepreneur of his or her

[8] Giovanni Maio, *Medizin ohne Maß. Vom Diktat des Machbaren zu einer Ethik der Besonnenheit* (Stuttgart: Trias, 2014).

own self and that we only need to choose the right instruments, in order to best utilise our »bio-capital«. As a result, every human problem appears unilaterally as a challenge to good management. We reduce people's problems to »management problems« and in so doing imply that whether the problem is solved depends solely on the individual, protracted or simply not »mastered«. This fundamental conviction of our time places the patients – and their therapists – under an almost unbearable pressure to succeed. Patients are made aware that they have to take care of the problem of pain in order to function smoothly again. This expectation is transferred onto the people treating the patient, so that they undertake to ensure that the pain is eliminated or abated in the end. Yet the less doctors and therapists succeed in suppressing the pain, the more patients become stricken with the idea of legitimacy. They describe their pain in ever more drastic detail so that it cannot be suggested they are only imagining it. In turn, the therapists feel even more powerless given that they cannot prevent the pain. This spiral can last for years: one examination follows the other, one method of treatment replaces the other, and always with the aim of sometime finally conquering the pain.[9]

However, in most cases this aim is misconceived. It is the objective of a world dominated by a control imperative. Above all, the imperative of control leaves patients with a feeling of failure and in some cases even of guilt. They feel personally responsible for the fact that they are still not free of pain, since they must have done something wrong or worse still have not yet succeeded in finding the right therapy, the right therapists, the right method.

---

[9] Marcus Schiltenwolf, »Medizin der Schmerzen – Divinum est dolorem sedare«, in *Die Schmerzen* ed. by M. Schiltenwolf and W. Herzog (Würzburg: Königshausen & Neumann, 2011), p. 143–159.

In principle, they *could* have achieved it, but they, in this particular case, have failed – this is the fateful credo lurking in the background. This credo is extremely dangerous because it leads to patients putting themselves under pressure and, bit by bit, dragging their therapists into this pressure too. The pressure to rid themselves of the pain at all costs, can, in the long term, lead to a fixation on the pain which in turn will completely disrupt their daily life. What, leads to the downfall of a patient suffering from pain is, therefore, not only the pain, but rather the idea, based on an ideology of practicability, that pain can be overcome if only the right method can be found. Only after years of living with pain do people come to the realisation that pain has a different characteristic when compared with other illnesses. We come to realise that pain cannot be fixed, but rather it can unwaveringly attach itself to life, making it impossible to find peace when we treat it as an enemy to be fought. Until this realisation takes hold, many patients must endure extremely painful experiences which pain inflicts on them.

Experiencing pain as a personal failure?

The most grave and aggravating experience with pain is the »experience of its uncontrollability«.[10] Recognising that a person is not in control of his or her pain is very difficult as it seems barely compatible with our perception of ourselves as autonomous beings. Every curative treatment of patients with chronic pain will remain unsuccessful without a concurrent treatment of their desire for control. It is extremely important to encourage patients to take the rational view that it

[10] Ursula Frede, *Herausforderung Schmerz* (Lengerich: Pabst, 2007), p. 43.

is not because of themselves, their will or their abilities that they cannot control the pain, but instead is down to the phenomenon of pain itself, which leads to the failure to control it. Even if it is not possible simply to relieve the patients of their chronic pain, it is, however, possible to at least release them from the feeling of personal failure. Patients with chronic pain feel under enormous pressure because they believe they are duty bound to society – their health insurance, their employer, and even their friends. They desperately cling to the mistaken idea they might somehow manage to keep their pain in check, as it is constantly implied that their pain is actually a treatable and controllable evil. The more they have this notion, the more they slide into a feeling of powerlessness, which not only gives them the feeling of helplessness, but on top of that the feeling of personal failure and guilt.

Captive and yet free – pain as a task to be overcome

What follows from all of this? As has already been shown, the basic problem of a number of treatments lies in the fact that they pursue an objective, which, as understandable as that may be, is, in most cases, destined to fail from the outset. In most cases, the unilateral aim – to fight against the pain – leads to the patient fighting not only against the pain, but also against life. By fixating on pain as an enemy to be constantly monitored, many people stifle the moments of freedom that would otherwise allow them to live their lives more fully (this phenomenon will be revisited in the chapter on cancer). As we have seen, pain spreads into a person's life and forces his or her life to deviate from that of a person who is not suffering from pain. However, by only fixating on the removal of pain, pain is given a scope and a power which it does not actually merit. The problem of the enemy metaphor is that pain takes on such an important role that people forget that, although they are people suffering from pain, they still have a scope of freedom beyond pain. Freedom for many patients with pain is not made impossible by the actual pain, but by their fear of it. It is important here that we work on not only dealing with pain but above all with the fear of pain. There is a time before pain and a time after. These times must not be completely taken up by pain, instead we must remain open to the experience that even in this time we still possess freedom.

Pain itself cannot be avoided. That is the nature of it. However, it is possible to prevent pain taking over our life in such a way that nothing else is possible. Pain compels us to adapt to a new life, but it is not the end of life; instead it is a task – the task of changing our lives in such a way that the remaining residuals of freedom can be accessed and accentuated. Thus, pain therapy cannot primarily mean fighting against the pain, but instead must mean a commitment to a life with pain. Pain is unwelcome. It is repugnant and we can never be reconciled to it. However, we can come to terms with it in that we can treat it, so to speak, as an unwelcome guest in our house with whom we can live even though we would prefer if they were to leave.[11] In order to learn to live with pain, we have to »tame« it which means we must reduce its influence on our lives. We must not allow it to exert its influence on our *whole* life. It inevitably has an impact, but only on a part of our life, not on our whole life. A person cannot control when pain comes any more than they can control whether they would like to have the pain or not: pain simply forces itself upon them without asking. However, they can control

---

[11] Ibid., p. 42 f.

the experience they have with this uninvited guest. They can control whether they experience the complete senselessness of life or whether the experience of pain makes them aware that they have resources which every human being possesses. Resources to curb the pain in one way or another and to resist its totalitising tendency, thus holding their own against the tyrant. This means holding their own, not in the way that the pain is controlled and prevented, but rather by showing the pain it is a house guest and not the house owner.

Against this background, meaningful treatment for a patient suffering from pain can only consist in giving them back that which pain and their social surroundings have taken away from: the feeling that their life has value, the feeling of having within themselves that they still have the capacity for action and freedom. Patients suffering from chronic pain are obliged to learn to trust in their future life with pain and not look back to a nostalgic and often romanticised view of life without pain.[12] Perhaps there will be a life without pain again, who knows. For the time being, a life with pain lies ahead, yet this life also leaves open degrees of freedom. These ideas only have to be tapped into and we must be open to the resources every human has within themselves which are often ignored, but which must first be brought to bear. This process is often only possible when guided by a professional who has learned to redefine the patient's treatment goals. This does not mean fighting against pain, but rather wrestling with a life with pain, a life which can be achieved once the credo of the fundamental idea of a contrivable world has been discarded. It is this thought which connects the important subject of pain with the next important theme, cancer, which will be discussed in the next chapter.

---

[12] Grüny, *Zerstörte Erfahrung*. Cp. , p. 175.

2. Cancer: Being excluded from normality

»The task of medical practice is not only to keep the sick alive, but also to keep them living a life.«

Almuth Sellschopp

Cancer – the very name strikes fear into the heart. It carries such metaphorical weight that the word itself engenders gloom and doom. To some extent, the word cancer still represents a kind of metaphor for death. The diagnosis of cancer is a traumatic event due to its association with immutable grief, lingering illness and dying. Against the background of a word with such strong connotations, when the word »malignant« is added, the expectation of calamity appears even more irrefutable. Cancer as something evil. The sociologist and medical historian Barbara Duden speaks critically of »oncophobia« and of »cancerisation« as a »specter of social disembodiment in a society of risk«.[1] This means that nothing good can come from cancer. In other words, the illness begins with this semantic burden; with this semantic burden one receives the diagnosis »cancer«. Yet we need not stop there: it is worth taking a closer look. What happens when a patient discovers he or she is suffering from the illness? What does it mean to be a cancer patient? In respect to medical practice based on care, cancer shows us how important it is to understand what

---

[1] Barbara Duden, »Die Verkrebsung: Kränkende Diagnostik durch Krebs-Prävention«, in: Ibid, *Die Gene im Kopf – der Fötus im Bauch. Historisches zum Frauenkörper.* (Hannover: Offizin-Verlag, 2002), pp. 166–186, here p. 167.

the patients themselves feel, experience, undergo and discover when they are confronted with the diagnosis. As Susan Sontag reflected in her famous essay, it is necessary »to show that illness is *not* a metaphor and that the most truthful way of regarding illness, and the healthiest way of being ill, is the one most purified of, most resistant to metaphoric thinking.«[2] Let us turn to seven points that address this theme.

1. The Diagnosis of Cancer: an abrupt break from normality

In his *Diary of a Cancer Patient,* the director Christoph Schlingensief expressed his feelings on being diagnosed with cancer very powerfully when he wrote: »Everything strikes me as being a separation. A separation from normality. This normality is violated and has abandoned me.«[3] This quote underlines how a cancer diagnosis strongly overrides everything and disrupts normality. Everything is turned upside down; it is as though the course of life has come to an abrupt halt and every support has been lost. Being diagnosed with cancer is initially traumatising because it breaks into one's life with such decisiveness and ruthlessness that it cannot be held at bay. It is simply impossible to evade, as it leaves no margin for interpretation. The diagnosis of cancer lays down facts which cannot be put into perspective. It makes people painfully aware that there is a life before the diagnosis and a

---

[2] Susan Sontag, *Krankheit als Metapher. Aus dem Amerikanischen von Karin Kersten und Caroline Neubaur.* (Munich: Hanser Verlag, 1977), p. 5.

[3] Christoph Schlingensief, *So schön wie hier kanns im Himmel gar nicht sein! Tagebuch einer Krebserkrankung.* (Cologne: Kiepenheuer & Witsch, 2009), p. 39.

life after, life amongst the healthy and life amongst the sick, and with the diagnosis the parameters have changed. They no longer belong to the realm of the healthy, which they had previously taken for granted, and instead are abruptly made aware of the fragility of their entire existence.

The significance of this realisation cannot be underestimated, for suddenly comparisons start to be made. Our present life is compared with our past life, our present consciousness with our light heartedness before the diagnosis, our present prospects with those that had somehow always been previously taken for granted. This adjustment is so painful that we are inevitably plunged into a deep crisis and into a state of instability and helplessness. This instability is evident in the fact that concepts of life which had previously been unconditionally accepted are now being questioned and what had previously been expected from life is now radically invalidated.

In the first instance, a diagnosis with cancer means a loss of support, as the patients are catapulted out of their previous normality and thrown into a strange world, where they are lost and seek in vain to find their way. The world in which the patients now find themselves turns out to be a precarious, unfamiliar and uprooted world. Many patients describe this state as »falling into a deep hole«, as plunging into complete helplessness. At that moment, precisely because they no longer have any idea of what they should do, they almost blindly submit themselves to a medical regime. This illustrates that a doctor's responsibility in this situation of a total loss of orientation cannot be underestimated.

2. Loss of control over one's life

The most harrowing thing about the diagnosis of cancer is, in the first instance, the feeling of losing control over one's own life. This diagnosis makes people painfully aware that their idea of a life that might be independently planned, and shaped down to the minutest detail, was an illusion. The diagnosis of cancer invalidates previously held life plans and shatters the expectation of continuity, where everything is planned and carries on as normal. This is the first thing that should be emphasised: we live with particular concepts of the future and with the belief that we ourselves determine these concepts of a good life. The whole time we are convinced that we hold life in our own hands and then the diagnosis of cancer strikes and does not allow life to be perceived as something actively manageable, but rather as something which takes away our control and which follows rules beyond our control.

The diagnosis draws people's attention, often for the first time, to their reliance on their body and necessitates a new understanding of themselves in which the illness is now what sets the pace and determines the future. In so doing, it inevitably changes people's perception of themselves and their relationship to their own body. Previously, in order to attain their goals, they had used their body in a casual way as an instrument, which operated as a vehicle of their own perception of a good life. With the diagnosis of cancer, the body takes charge, so to speak, makes demands and intervenes in their life plans. A person diagnosed with cancer reacts painfully to their physical condition, for the cancer draws attention to their body and relentlessly demands that henceforth their whole attention be focused on it.

In this respect, cancer is somewhat special, as it makes people aware that it is not an outside agent, a bacterium, a poison or an accident which has attacked the body, but rather it is their own body cells which have brought about the threat. With cancer in their body, a person has, for the first time, a sense of hostility, of unpredictability and even malice. And the more this view of the own body is internalised, the more they distance themselves from it and become alienated from it. Against this background, we can after all make sense of and understand why many patients submit to chemotherapy treatment. For in the face of a radical loss of control, chemotherapy treatment provides a platform for fighting back against the perceptions of the cancer's control and power; for as long as sick people fight, they do not have the impression that they are giving in, and have the feeling of »attacking« the cancer when almost everyone knows that this battle cannot be won. The fight is simply a counter balance to the unbearable loss of control over our life.

3. Loss of bodily security

Having cancer is therefore a profound experience because it changes one's identity. This change begins with one's body feeling alien. The impact of the diagnosis spells a premature end to the feeling of self-security within oneself. The body loses its previous naturalness because it has conceived something which could not be felt and was also unexpected. Now the people affected are living inside a body which is now inherently unpredictable. Their own body has become an alien body, of which they need to be wary. This wariness and the constant fear that something new could grow inside spells an end to the intimacy with their own body. This loss of intimacy relates not only to the conceivable possibility of a recurrence, a hidden metastasis, or other relapses, but also to the fact that one's own body is no longer as reliable as it used to be. Cancer goes hand in hand with wild fluctuations; sometimes patients are full of energy, sometimes completely exhausted, and they never know what tomorrow will bring. Their body dictates new rules, which never become completely clear. It simply removes the accustomed order.

Seeing themselves confronted not only with the loss of their accustomed order and with the loss of intimacy with their body, but also with the loss of being able to rely on their physical state is one of the gravest experiences of a person with cancer. When someone's body becomes more and more alien and unpredictable, something occurs which must be described as a break in identity, a break resulting in the loss of unity between the self and the body. The I and the body are now perceived to be separated, as if the body were under alien influence. It is no longer the patients' own mental state which imprints their being upon their body, but an alien entity, the illness, which ruthlessly impresses its own rules onto the body. Consequently, this new relationship to their body is no longer a relationship of comfort and intimacy, but instead a relationship of being kept in check, a relationship of feeling threatened by oneself, and a relationship of deep anxiety. Maxie Wander memorably expressed this feeling in her book: *Leben wär' eine prima Alternative* (*Life Would Be A Super Alternative*) using the following metaphor: »Thinking about cancer, it's like being locked in a dark room with a murderer. You don't know where, how and if they will attack you.«[4] Or to put it another way: something which previously had been considered a part of oneself, becomes, due to the unpredictable illness, something alien, something which now must be permanently and continually brought under control. This co-

---

[4] Maxie Wander, *Leben wär' eine prima Alternative. Tagebücher und Briefe*, ed. by Fred Wander. (Frankfurt am Main: Suhrkamp, 2009), p. 18.

incides with the experience of the body altering in a way which evades one and forces one into a new body pattern, which poses a special challenge to integrate this idiosyncratic being into one's own concept of life.

This particular challenge often means that daily routine can itself become a burden. If someone feels, due to the physical effects of cancer, that managing previously easy tasks becomes more and more like having to contend with almost insurmountable obstacles, they radically retreat into themselves. Even the smallest undertaking becomes a mammoth task, which must be meticulously planned down to the minutest detail and every possible thing that could go wrong. When even getting on a train or going to the bakery becomes a major challenge, there is a danger of becoming isolated since this narrowing of boundaries often leads to a loss of power when facing these tasks, inspite of the size of the obstacles.

Moreover, with daily tasks becoming more and more difficult, the physical manifestation of the illness becomes evident and something is lost which previously was not perceived as something of value, namely the possibility of anonymity, the possibility to disappear into the crowd and to remain, so to speak, invisible to those around us in everyday life. On the one hand, physical manifestations may paralyse someone but on the other hand, they become unmistakable for others who are immediately taken aback by these physical changes and totally change their behaviour towards the sick person. There are people, who, out of sheer uncertainty, do not know how they should speak to someone and so would rather act as if they did not see them. They treat them as someone to be avoided and stigmatised. Then there are others who are aghast, show pity and ask questions. It also becomes increasingly impossible to hold a »normal« conversation with cancer patients. Everything is now concentrated on the visible physical signs; people with cancer suddenly stand out from the crowd of »normal healthy people«. They are singled out and can no longer casually interact with those around them, as the »stigmas« are suddenly pushed centre stage. When situations become more frequent where they are suddenly confronted with questions or only subjected to glances, every undertaking turns out to be a twofold challenge: the challenge of simply accomplishing a task physically and at the same time the challenge of being in contact with people who almost automatically tend to interrupt their path and involve them in conversation.

Normality is doubly suspended, both in relation to overcoming everyday situations as well as in relation to everyday interaction. The danger may well arise from this that a person who has cancer is not only subjected to adversities, but also increasingly avoids confrontation, owing to this break in normality, and so withdraws socially. People with cancer are in danger of social isolation, not only due to the fact that they are restricted in their freedom of movement and their ability to cope with daily life, but also because it is made impossible for them to feel normal because of and in spite of their illness.

4. Farewell to the Reliability of the Future

The challenge of being diagnosed with cancer does not just lie in losing the prospect of a rich perspective of the future, it is more than that. The future will be robbed not only of its breadth but also of its predictability, its calculability and even its dependability. Cancer comes with a fundamental threat which will not go away. in this way, the future not only becomes more restricted, but above all less plannable. You start something without knowing whether you will be able to finish it. In the first instance this has a paralysing effect. Again and again the question arises: Is it still worth it? What is in fact worth it at all? This is also the reason why almost every doctor treating oncology patients is constantly confronted with the question: »How long do I have?« That sounds like: How much of my life do I have to cut off? And yet the tragedy does not simply lie in having to cut life short, hence in the loss of time, it also lies in the change of perspective and the change in the time still remaining. The time remaining is time of a completely different nature. It is essentially more inaccessible than the time previously anticipated; it is something which can no longer be factored in and precisely because of this becomes, to a certain extent, »extra time«. Time has lost its implicitness but for that very reason it can become a time of gratefulness and appreciation. As tragic as the diagnosis is, it changes everything, above all one's own attitude to time and consequently to the world, it leaves the door open for the feeling of humility, because it must be recognised that the time which lies ahead cannot itself simply be tied down and controlled. It can only be hoped for (see Chapter 7).

Something fundamental becomes apparent here. Life with cancer has the character of ambivalence. On the one hand, there is the gratitude for every day that can be lived and yet on the other hand the dull underlying feeling of fear, fear of an uncertain future and fear of all that might lie ahead. This uncertainty and unpredictability of what the future might hold can be a nagging feeling, which can make a person incapable of action and can plunge them into inner resignation. Due to this deep-seated fear of the future, cancer ultimately has the effect of pointing people towards the present. A person suffering from cancer, as almost no other, lives in the present. The view to the future is obscured by its unpredictability and looking back to the past is often so painful that it is avoided. Looking back to a time of living in a carefree way, without actually knowing *how* carefree it was hurts deeply because the realisation dawns that this time is gone once and for all. Looking into the past is like looking at a time when one was a completely different person and this is now painful because that time is irretrievably lost. The irretrievable past and the unmanageable future point people suffering from cancer towards the here and now, for this is the only thing which they can understand, the only thing they can practically deal with and the only thing which remains a tangible reality. And yet the painful reminder of the finite nature of their own life spurs them on to evaluate their past life. The experience of cancer is both a powerful experience of the present and, at the same time, an experience of a desire to take stock of a life lived, an experience of searching for the substance of one's life which will outlive one's physical existence.

5. Metamorphosis

The experience of having cancer is initially devastating and destructive. It is, above all, a destruction of a previously planned future and of prospects which had previously seemed self-evident. It also signifies the disruption of previously valid points of orientation. It initially leads to a loss of orientation and to a life which, it is believed, plunges into nothingness. A cancer diagnosis constitutes a fall from one's previously accustomed life, a fall from its certainty and being cast out of a state of obliviousness. Being cast out of this life that had been taken for granted is a major crisis, and it is unclear what there will be at the end of this crisis. Initially what prevails is anger, emptiness and a future which has become an illusion. Yet life continues and this continuing life transforms into a state of learning, but time is needed in order to leave the state of helplessness and to learn to live anew. To learn to live afresh is only possible, if one succeeds in accepting a future that it can no longer be planned as before. This new life is a life of hesitantly approaching an intangible future, a future which cannot be controlled but which can merely be taken as it comes. At this juncture, hesitancy takes centre stage. Slowly a person grows into an understanding of themselves which allows them to also accept the intangible as it is and yet find new direction within this intangible future. At first, one simply does not want to think about what will happen in the next few years, as this creates fear. Yet with every new day which the person experiences, they realise that life does somehow go on and that there is indeed a future, be it simply the future of a new week they can experience. The person does not want to think about what the situation will be in a year's time but this one week was real. So as the next week approaches the patient accepts it, hesitantly, but with an ever growing conviction that, even with this uncertain future, it is possible to exist, to live, and to experience profound feelings.

During the course of the illness, what takes place is nothing less than a metamorphosis, in fact a metamorphosis of future goals culminating in a metamorphosis of one's own personality. At the beginning of the illness people initially hit rock bottom; it is not possible to set new goals at this stage, for all security is shattered and they find themselves in a state of total inexperience. They have never experienced such a situation before and have no idea what is in front of them and how things will move forward, as the illness and its progression appear completely alien to them. Initially they must familiarise themselves with it and gather experiences to even become capable of action. Though the future may, therefore, initially seem to be out of their control, they do learn, in time, to recognise how to manage their short-term future within a longer-term future that has become uncertain, and to operate within it. This represents an incisive experience which cancer imposes on someone, namely the experience that it is not possible to actively shape everything by oneself, but that, from now on, *what* can be shaped takes on an entirely new value. The loss of scope for the future is accompanied by an appreciation of the possibilities of the here and now.

Time is more limited, planning more difficult, but the time remaining is approached consciously. It is, in a sense, refined by the awareness of reduced time. In this sense, the illness can almost operate as a catalyst in the form of a vital impulse towards a new beginning. In this way, it appears in its biformity as both a traumatising life event and at the same time an opportunity for development. Due to the illness, the breadth of the temporal horizon is lost and yet depth is gained. Depth arises from a more conscious life and from the much more conscious choice of one's own preferences, but also relationships. People affected by cancer are more particular and selective. They now recognise certain relationships or activities as meaningless which were previously simply accepted, and concentrate on what is really important to them. Awareness of time changes, and dealing with their time, which has become more precious, takes on a new character. The awareness of being seriously ill leads to a person focusing on everything they hold dear. In this regard, cancer acts as a magnifying glass which unfailingly identifies what a person holds close to their heart. Out of this heightened awareness grows the will to shape one's own life. The following unforgettable words on this attitude towards life come from the previously cited work, *Maxie Wander – Leben wär' eine prima Alternative (Life Would Be A Super Alternative)*: »I will savour every drop of life. Life in small doses.

But I'm sure I'll get more out of my life than other people who don't know what life really is!«[5]

For some people, the illness represents the very first conscious attempt to shape their life according to self-defined aims and to organise it according to requirements which come from within themselves and not from mere convention. This is arguably what Heidegger described as »authentic« life: the detaching from inauthenticity, from life enslaved to what »one« does. A person suffering from cancer no longer lives as »one« lives. Their life is more conscious, more self-determined and more target-oriented. They live out what they actually deem to be important. This inevitably leads to a more in-depth analysis and an often radical new assessment of their previous life. In a certain sense, cancer is a ruthless interrogator. It questions sufferers' earlier life and often, when faced with cancer, they recognise shortcomings in the focus and structure of their former life, which had previously been indiscernible. Sometimes, for the first time, a painful consciousness arises of what has not been lived – sorrow for an unlived life. However, hand in hand with this experience of loss goes an »experience of winning«, as the cancer leads to a heightened sensitivity to what is going on all around, processes and realities, and which previously had not been perceived at all. Many cancer patients report that, with the illness, they experienced things occurring in nature, for example, which in the past they had completely overlooked. Hence, a plant beginning to grow in their garden can thrill patients in a previously unimaginable way. The illness sensitises and opens our eyes. It also opens our eyes in that moment and in so doing makes possible an experience which can be more profound than any ecstasy. Maxi Wander encapsulates this perfectly when she writes: »Only when you have

[5] Ibid., p. 45.

grasped how quickly you can be taken and how precious our one and only unrepeatable life is, do you begin to live.«[6]

The illness highlights the present as being valuable in itself without comparing it with the past and the future. It can enable many people to recognise the preciousness of the moment for the first time and consciously to face the present in a way which had previously been thought impossible. The illness causes a shift in standards and also a change in demands. In many people the experience of cancer has the effect of putting their demands on life into perspective. In a certain sense they become less demanding because they learn to accept the limits which have been imposed on them and thus learn to transfer their hopes to other things. This was repeatedly expressed by Christoph Schlingensief with his typical inimitable clarity: »Only when we surrender and let things happen do we discover the freedom we have. It is of course a paradoxical idea: Only at the very moment of a radical lack of freedom do we discover true freedom.«[7] Schlingensief rightly concludes that only by freeing life from demands, can the depth of life be fully understood and appreciated. Furthermore, only when people who are seriously ill learn not to fixate on beating cancer at all costs and on having to get better at all costs, do they gain the freedom of recognising what possibilities still lie ahead in their life with the illness. By reducing their demands, they will be able to stamp their own mark on their present life and do what corresponds with their person – and that is real freedom.

---

[6] Ibid.

[7] Christoph Schlingensief, *So schön wie hier kanns im Himmel gar nicht sein!* (Cologne: Kiepenheuer & Witsch, 2009), p. 129.

6. Recognising hidden resources

In their more conscious life, people who have become ill realise that they have resources they can draw on, which only now have become clear to them. This is the paradox of being ill: something is lost and at the same time a new consciousness of being able to conquer adversity is gained. The adversities show people their ability to cope, which had been unnoticed before. This reminds me of a story by Michael Ende in which he introduces the figure of the illusory giant who only looks like a giant from a distance, yet the closer one gets to him, the more he shrinks to a normal size. Cancer is like this illusory giant. As we established earlier, from a distance »cancer« sounds like the revelation of calamity, powerlessness and immeasurable sorrow. This distance is the healthy person's view of the illness. For healthy people, the possibility of becoming ill with cancer represents a total catastrophe. But the people who actually suffer from the illness have to endure these feelings, feelings which lead to doubt and also sometimes to despair. If, however, they receive support and come through this phase, the insurmountable giant that is cancer will increasingly turn into an illusory giant. Cancer becomes part of their normality and transports them to a place of new insight about themselves, which can evoke its own form of support. Suddenly they are amazed how they were able to overcome this, they are amazed at the strength which was lying dormant in themselves and amazed that they are not broken. This feeling of not being broken by adversity can become something very supportive because they see themselves as well equipped to brave the future. They may well have to endure a future with physical discomfort and disabilities, but it will be a future that belongs to no-one else but them. They themselves will shape this future in their own way. Suddenly the realisation grows that, in spite of being subjected to it, they can still shape this future.

7. Re-establishing normality

It takes time to find ways of escaping from this feeling of being helpless and at the mercy of cancer, and to recognise that there are numerous ways to react individually to the illness, to cancer. If the person with cancer is well cared for normality can be re-established, but it will be one with only few remaining parallels to that normality which determined life before the outbreak of illness. This new normality is the result of a transition, the result of a new orientation and a rediscovery of life within a fragmented life. Medical practice focuses, often too one-sidedly, on functions which have become lost and so fails to understand that a life affected by cancer also continues to have healthy components right to its end. A life damaged by cancer does not have to be perceived as being damaged, but can be seen as a phase of transition to a new health, a form of health which no longer emphasises that everything is possible, but rather emphasises the increased awareness of the value of the things that are still possible. Our view changes and becomes more penetrating and with this enhanced focus allows us to discover the fullness in a life which a superficial observer would simply reduce to being a damaged life. A full life in fragments. This is the re-establishment of normality in a life with cancer, even if the cancer is incurable. This new orientation can help the patients regain consciousness to once more become the »conductor« of their own life and not have to surrender completely to the »baton« of their illness. This path is an arduous one and above all a mental path, but if they succeed, they discover degrees of freedom within this insurmountable illness. The illness itself cannot be beaten, but the structure that life takes with the illness is still in one's own hands. However, the scope for shaping one's own life only opens up when one has freed oneself of the notion of the good life lead as a healthy person. We are encouraged to seek out new points of orientation, to find new content, and to detect new meaningful reasons – and suddenly we realise that we do not have to be free of cancer to feel the richness of life, to experience the preciousness of the moment, and to joyfully experience an encounter with nature, other people, or art and literature. Becoming ill forces people to find new and meaningful values for themselves and these can be found, if people feel inclined to look for them and if they do not have to look for them entirely on their own. Some people rebel in their illness, others feel guilt, others give up initially, and yet they all have something in common: without fail they all embark on a search. They look for new goals, also for explanations, but above all for goals which can give meaning to their existence.

Cancer constitutes a shock, above all a shock to one's own self and a shock to previous self-conceptions. Because of this, previous concepts of one's own life story begin to crack, and this requires a re-telling of this story, in order to give life a different direction and create a completely different entity. Real help for people with cancer can only therefore consist in seeing that the shock of getting the illness has the potential for growth, growth which leads to a new awareness of life. This requires a re-telling of the individual's life story so that the break in normality caused by the illness does not represent the termination of life but instead the breakthrough to a new design of life. In the end, this possibly says more about one's own identity than all the life plans that had been formulated and followed when healthy.

All in all, it seems important to bear in mind that the first reaction to a diagnosis of cancer is initially an attempt to reach security and stability by holding on tightly to established mechanisms. Hence, the first step in the struggle against cancer consists in enhancing all strategies for its elimination, in order to recapture this »damaged« (Schlingensief) normality. At the beginning, we focus on the illness. We declare it our enemy and implicitly assume that life can only continue when this enemy is defeated. However, the more we remain focused in this way, the more improbable will be our life *with* cancer. For having an enemy means we are constantly aware of this fact and have to expend all our energy controlling it in such a way that we no longer pay attention to life itself. This initial revolt is a completely natural reaction; of course, we want to hold on to what is tried and tested and to try everything to rid ourselves of this disruptive element cancer, which has so abruptly interrupted our life, so that life can flow again as normal. However, it is equally important to recognise this phase as an initial state of shock and to resist being trapped by it. In other words, this would mean nothing less than suppressing the possibilities of an interpersonal life by focusing on the worries of a biological continuation of life.

As long as we only look at biological life, we neglect all the life that is indeed threatened, but still exists in the here and now with its spiritual wealth, self-knowledge and interpersonal experience. This is equally true for both people who are ill and those surrounding them. However, for the treatment of a person affected by cancer, this can only mean that this first phase – the fight for biological life – is to be overcome at some point. From the moment when the cancer can no longer be beaten, this should be recognised as a transitionary phase. The re-establishment of the accustomed flow should now no longer take centre stage, but rather the adjustment of the flow to a new concept of a successful life. Initially the illness is fought off; this is entirely natural, but no-one can really live in a purely resistive mode. Therefore, it is important to replace resistance with support and integration. It is important to free oneself from this »contra« mode at some point, and rediscover the »pro« mode. This distortive doggedness to fight the illness must be replaced as early as possible by a realistic commitment to one's own life with cancer. At the very latest from the moment when the illness is recognised as incurable, it must be integrated into one's own concept of life in such a way that it does not remain a pervasive and overshadowing factor, but instead has its place in a biography that continues in spite of cancer and yet at the same time takes a new course. This course may be shorter and yet can lead to a new and hitherto unknown fulfilment.

We have now considered two major issues in modern medical practice, pain and cancer, which are linked by the fundamental idea of the possibility of not living *against* them but instead living *with* them. Both chronic pain and cancer constituted challenges to our own approach to them, and both revealed that it is important to recognise our own potential and to learn a way of dealing with them that enhances our life. Dementia, our next topic, is a challenge of a different kind, because the main point here is how society, close relatives, and professional helpers approach it. Dementia, namely an illness where we can still be ourselves, yet no longer without the help of a third party. This is the theme of the next chapter.

3. Dementia: Why we can learn a lot about ourselves from people suffering from dementia

> »Dementia does not evoke a special form of being human, but rather requires special conditions of communication.«
>
> *Dominik A. Becker*

I was recently speaking to a friend who I had not seen for a very long time. When I asked her about the health of an elderly relative who we had both known, she answered: »She is still alive, but, unfortunately, she has dementia and it's not possible to have a conversation with her anymore, so I haven't been to visit her for a long time.« Her answer made me think. The old lady is still alive and yet for my friend she is somehow already dead. This corresponds to a widely held perception of this illness: dementia as a farewell to the self, as a farewell to what to everything that has made a person who he or she is.

This idea shocks a lot of people and consequently dementia has become a horror scenario in our society, and we believe the only response is to react with a death wish, assisted suicide and radical resistance. The reason for this hatred of dementia is its direct identification with the loss of self. We must reflect more carefully on this point if we want to do justice to the phenomenon of dementia. Reflecting does not mean glossing over it or trivialising it: the diagnosis of dementia is a traumatic blow, something that cannot be turned into something positive. However, life with dementia, life with a person with dementia, life with the awareness of the inexorable progression of the illness, is not simply a non-life, a life to be avoided at all costs. It is still a life and, in the best case, a life in continuing companionship, a life that must not simply become what cannot be, but rather one which can be seen to have its own vitality, its own biography and in a certain sense its own self.

In the first instance, it is important to realise what the diagnosis of dementia means to a person. We associate the loss of the ability to remember and the breakdown of intellectual powers with this illness and yet it is much more than that. Dementia is not only a conglomeration of symptoms, it is a diagnosis which devastates the whole person because it affects the whole person like no other diagnosis. Telling a person for the first time that he or she will have to live with dementia ranks among the most sensitive situations for a doctor. Any attempts to find something positive in the illness are doomed to failure. Dementia is a tragedy. It cannot be glossed over, not romanticised and not brushed aside with false platitudes of pity. The diagnosis is and remains a bitter shock for the person affected and possibly to an even greater extent to immediate family members, regardless of the situation in which the patients, their family and their dependents find themselves.

The tragedy of dementia lies in the fact that one feels totally at the mercy of the illness. With so many other illnesses there is initially hope, hope for relief, even perhaps a cure, certainly in any case hope for some form of recovery. Dementia offers none of these. There is no hope of a cure, there is no hope that »it« will get better. In no way will it get better. The only remaining hope is slowing down the progression of the illness, stopping it is impossible, at least not in the foreseeable future. Recognising this is extremely difficult, as the feeling of helplessness is one which no-one wants to surrender to. Yet life with dementia is not a life which leaves no room for hope. The purpose of this section is to demonstrate this.

In medical practice there has long been an attempt to regard dementia as an illness which is objectively diagnosed and clinically treated. This is the typical approach of medical practice to phenomena in the world, but this approach is – not only with respect to dementia – all too one-sided, as necessary as it may otherwise be. For dementia is not only an objective illness, it is at the same time a form of human existence that is suffered subjectively. People with dementia live as *people* and not as dementia patients. It is true their life is determined by dementia, but it is not subsumed by it, because people with dementia are above all people and so remain distinctive and unique individuals in spite of their illness. It is important not only to ask how dementia negatively affects a person, but also above all what the illness means to all the people concerned and how their lives will be affected by dementia. Let us therefore consider this phenomenon of life more closely and attempt to establish a small »phenomenology of dementia«.

The obstructed approach to one's own history

My friend's reaction underlines the fact that dementia patients are often treated by family members as if they no longer have a personality or their own self, as if their very being had disappeared along with their memory and their mental capability. This can already be understood from the term dementia (from the Latin *mens*, »mind« and *de-*, »from, away«), which simply says that people who are victims of this illness have forfeited their faculty of thought, their mind and indeed their character. However, this linguistic connotation is deceptive. Dementia patients lose something; that is undisputed. But in the first instance it is not their memory that they lose. In fact, they lose the mental access to their memory. How is this to be understood? Whoever has dealings with Alzheimer patients will soon notice that they are just as unique as people who are not ill: each person enjoys something different and each person suffers with something different. Of course, they have similar symptoms; they all initially lose the cognitive capacity to recall experiences from their early lives and all quickly have difficulties recognising familiar people. However, we all too quickly draw the conclusion from this missing ability that dementia patients have lost their memory. Those who work closely with them will recognise that they are full of memories. A piece of music from the past can spontaneously awaken feelings and emotionally transport the person back to past times; a scent from their childhood involuntarily reawakens memories. Close relatives of dementia patients experience this »awakening« almost every day. It is clear from this that dementia patients are actually not dementia patients, but rather cryptomnesia patients: their memories are not simply erased, they are merely buried and hidden, concealed and more difficult to access. The life of a person with Alzheimer's is primarily shaped by discontinuity. It is the missing connection between earlier and present-day events which characterises their experience. Dementia patients continually have new experiences and so lose the feeling of historical continuity in their biography. That appears to us as outsiders to be a narrative disruption in the story of their life; however, we fail thereby to recognise that the ability to experience remains, as well as the basic ability to retrieve old information in spite of a lack of coherence. Current experience is not assimilated into a new historical entity, but remains fragmentary. The experience of a person with an illness of this type can thus be described as an experience in fragments, in intensive fragments, which can no longer be bundled into a coherent life story.

Effectively, this discontinuation is nothing more than the lost ability to behave reflexively towards oneself. Dementia patients lose the possibility of a cognitive self-reference, but this does not mean that they no longer have an identity. It is true that they cannot rationally access earlier identities and connect them with present ones, but they still have an identity: they sense, feel, think, but they always think and feel in the here and now. That is the particularity of dementia, always being in the here and now, without a connection to the past and without anticipation of the future. There certainly remains some form of self-reference, but it is not a cognitive one, but rather a physical self-reference, a consciousness of one's own self as a physical certainty of being here. This makes the fragments of real feelings which reveal themselves to be are even more valuable. Even if they cannot be assimilated into a whole, they remain emotive expressions of a momentary feeling and through the validity of these feelings in the given situation they become something precious, something worth encouraging and developing.

Moreover, what the patients feel *now*, despite its fragmentary character, is related to earlier experiences. Earlier experiences are certainly not erased, they are only no longer connected with present day experiences in a rational way to form a story. But they are still present. Every person with dementia reacts on the basis of earlier experiences, since these experiences have etched themselves in him or her as a physical experience, even if no conscious access to them is now possible. Earlier experiences are, so to speak, the atmospheric platform on which present reactions are built. Therefore, what was previously experienced remains the core of the person's personality, and this in turn also has something continuous, regardless of disruptions.

Therefore, the appropriate way of dealing with people with dementia can only be to enable them scope to newly discover situational experiences without wanting to unite these single experiences into a single entity. It is about embarking on a journey to free buried experiences and memories from within the patient and allow them, one by one, to come to life. It is only in this way that cryptomnesia patients can repeatedly become *re*mentia patients, who rediscover their memory time and time again and can, therefore, constantly gain new experiences. It is important here that we do not fall into the trap of *restitutio*: when working with dementia patients it cannot be a case of »restoring« something, of bringing something back to its original place, or of bringing the patients back to their former condition. Alzheimer's is a journey which cannot end in a healthier place than at its outset but it is also not a journey which simply leads into darkness. It will indeed become darker. This has to be acknowledged and any attempt to trivialise the inaccessibility of the past appears cynical in the face of the despair which, at the beginning, often not only affects the patient's close circle but also the patient. However, people with Alzheimer's do not have to remain in despair, if it is explained to them that they have resources which enable them to repeatedly rekindle a part of their earlier experiences and thus repeatedly feel alive.

Above all, patients with dementia must not be weighed down with trying to be as before, or feeling the need to achieve something. They must be allowed to build a new world around them. A world which they assimilate with other feelings, with other forms of consciousness and where they react in a new and unprecedented fashion. They are no longer rooted in their former patterns of behaviour and yet they still behave as a unique and distinctive individuals. Conversations with them will sometimes even be more open and relaxed, as there will be no role expectations and their reactions will be more instantaneous. This was wonderfully illustrated by Tilman Jens when he wrote about the relationship with his father Walter Jens who was suffering from dementia: »I have discovered a completely different father, a natural father, who simply laughs when he sees me, who cries a lot and just moments later is delighted with a piece of cake or a glass of cherry juice.«[1] Dementia has given a new uninhibitedness to Tilman Jens' relationship to his father.

This new relationship of uninhibitedness is, however, only conceivable if we bear in mind that the patients are, strictly speaking, not dementia patients, but people who have quite certainly retained their memories, yet now need support in order to grasp them and find new access to them. This uncovering of memory can then no longer be a rational uncovering; it is not just a matter of producing chronicity or attaching the correct connections. Uncovering here would be much more associative, something related to feeling. Memories can be awakened by access to a patient's emotions. Dementia patients have their previous experiences etched into their still enduring personality and it is now no longer reason which leads them to these deep levels of memory, it is physical experience. It is the scent of their favourite flower, the sound of a piece of music, the sensation of being caressed, the feel of the sun or the taste of chocolate. It is these corporeal and sensory impressions which, for Alzheimer patients, can pave the way to a new access to their submerged memories. However, they must be given the opportunity to make such sensory experiences.

People with dementia suffer the loss of cognitive abilities, but they retain access to the world through their body. They retain the ability to perceive their own body and hence also to

---

[1] Tilman Jens. *Demenz. Abschied von meinem Vater* (Munich: Goldmann, 2010) p. 133.

feel comfortable in themselves and to experience feelings of pleasure. It is simply important to be interested in these people, to give them access to these pleasurable feelings in their bodies, whether it be the pleasant feeling of warm water, the pleasant feeling of something soft or the warm feeling of the tenderness of a gesture. It was therefore tragic when my friend suggested that there was really no point in visiting her relative suffering from dementia. She took away the possibility for her to have new experiences and to lead her to hidden memories in her life through bodily sensations.

The veil of unfamiliarity

Bearing in mind that deep within a person there is memory, but that it cannot be consciously awakened and that all impressions that arise in the present are not cognitively connected to this buried memory, one thing becomes clear: people suffering from dementia must feel infinitely alienated from themselves, in an alien world cut off from everything that was once familiar. They are living in their familiar environment, but they no longer recognise this familiarity and their visual impressions are no longer connected to their deeper layers of self. *Everything* has become alien to them. What is missing here on an existential level is the feeling of security. The anxiety, restless wandering, and sometimes even aggression of many Alzheimer's patients can be interpreted as expressions of this loss of security and of searching for a reliable support. Comfort and security are lost since the patients can no longer perceive their previously familiar surroundings as a trusted environment. By losing the ability to establish a connection between their present impressions and their past experiences, they suddenly find their home a strange place, since the bridge between now and before becomes progressively fragile. What happened before is indeed still there, but is not being automatically accessed by seeing a former familiar face, but rather via indirect paths.

Recently, I was treating an elderly lady suffering from dementia who was living in a prestigious care home near Freiburg. She was led into a room where her daughter was waiting for her, but whom she did not recognise as her daughter. When her daughter, who was very sensitive and had always enjoyed a very good relationship with her mother, stroked her gently on the arm as she had always done, the patient said: »Just like my Anna«. Her daughter Anna could, therefore, still offer her comfort, but it was not enough simply to be there. Rather, she first had to remind herself of the past, in order, via tactile stimuli, to make the past also accessible to her mother. It was necessary to take an indirect route via the body of her mother, via sensory stimuli and new associations.

Patients with dementia lose the feeling of security because reality as it is presented to them is no longer self-evident. They are living in a reality which they consider alien, because it is perceived to be detached from their previous experiences, even though it was a part of their own biography. What was previously a matter of course becomes ever more unfamiliar; a person with dementia experiences the reality surrounding them through a veil of unfamiliarity. But it is only a veil behind which this familiar world still exists. First, however, access to it must be found, a new access which is only possible together with other people. That is why helping dementia patients primarily involves helping them rediscover what used to be familiar and helping them lift the veil of unfamiliarity.

The shame of disappointing others

An Alzheimer's diagnosis inevitably comes as a shock, not only for relatives but also for the person concerned. This shock is a huge challenge. It eats away at self-esteem and triggers fears, some of which are sometimes unbearable. The worst thing about this fear at the beginning of the illness is the dread of letting one's loved ones down. Resulting from this fear, which in the first year constantly accompanies people with dementia like no other, is the feeling of shame. They live in »shame mode« because they are ashamed of not being able to do certain things anymore and ashamed of the disappointments they believe they are inflicting on their loved ones. Their shame makes them feel increasingly lonely and distraught because they believe they have to live up to the expectations of others, who still treat them as the person they were before, and to the expectations they have of being and of behaving as before.

In order to help patients with Alzheimer's, the most effective approach seems to me to be not constantly to confront them with what they can no longer do, not to correct and reprimand them, but rather to show them *all the things they can still do.* In this way, we give them new self-esteem and simply through appreciative care and understanding, we take away the oppressive fear of shame. For shame does not arise from inability; shame arises from the internalisation of a social expectation.

This implicit expectation can be worked on every day by practising giving back self-esteem to dementia patients who are still kind people who have something to say to us, precisely by being themselves and by the way they deal with their own frailty. The feeling of shame must be offset by a culture of esteem, for shame is destructive in the long run. It gradually leads to »inner exile« and thus to extreme loneliness. Shame evokes withdrawal tendencies and thus is a feeling of desocialisation, which poses an extreme threat to dementia patients in particular. It is, however, treatable: it »only« takes one person to bestow security through a caring approach. Relationships which create a feeling of security are the antidote and the most powerful remedy for destructive shame. It is worth considering how we can reflect back to patients all the things they can still do, how much they can still decide for themselves, and how much of their former ability is still lying dormant within them. The most important thing is communicating appreciation and recognition and to this end small gestures that convey a positive resonance are required. Why not enable dementia patients to take part in painting, singing, or making things? Why not demonstrate to them their creativity which still remains? Why not show them that we still want to ask them about things, whether it is simply about their favourite flavour of ice cream or what their preferred daily routine would be?

The ability to resonate

A basic mistake in dealing with people with dementia is that we always look at what they can no longer do and so it is easy to overlook what they can still do. The most fundamental and important of their remaining abilities is, without doubt, communication with others. People suffering from dementia still communicate with the people around them, they simply communicate in a different way. It is no longer communication via the discursive exchange of information, but rather a much more primal understanding by means of a pre-reflexive detection of atmosphere. After a certain point, dementia patients can no longer elucidate and reason, but they can sense and express themselves in a sensual way by absorbing the atmosphere and being carried along by it. People with dementia can be stimulated, they can be taken along and can be filled with enthusiasm, provided they are given not only the right thing to *do*, but are also provided with the right atmosphere. Dementia patients sense more than we realise, and it is precisely this which makes them so special: their sensibility remains intact, in fact if anything it increases and leaves them more sensitive than healthy people. Patients with dementia sense feelings floating in the air, they sense the impatience of the person opposite them, they sense disinterest, they sense human sympathy and they sense the tenderness of a glance, just as they also sense the boredom of the person sitting across from them. Dementia patients feel all of this. It is the sensitivity of the spoken voice that communicates the message and not the material content. So if we do not visit them because we cannot converse with them, we disregard this deep intuition and miss out on communicating with them, which no longer consists of words, but of looking, touching, singing and simply passing time. People with dementia speak to us constantly because they have the ability to resonate with us. An ability which we should possibly relearn ourselves; not only in order to understand dementia patients, but also to rediscover ourselves as human beings. Is it not the case that intonation and pitch are often more important than the content in a conversation, in receiving what has been said? The way in which dementia patients react reminds us of the significance of paraverbal communication.

Life in Relation

The more one works with people affected by dementia the clearer it becomes: even though they may lose the ability to act consistently and to interact with the world discursively, they still remain receptive to the outside world. It is not only the aforementioned ability to resonate, which distinguishes them, it is more than that: it is the consistency in their relation to others, which we can experience daily with them. People suffering from dementia still relate to other people, but they do not do this through verbal communication, but via the body. It is their body which experiences, and their body which feels affection or rejection. People with dementia communicate physically by reacting with anxiety when they feel themselves left alone, and with almost childlike pleasure when they feel affection, remember wonderful experiences or find appreciation. They encourage us to communicate with them via their physical existence; and in doing so it is not their word but their body which requires an interpersonal reaction. A person with dementia reminds us again that body language is a language which we have almost forgotten.

Patients with dementia express themselves physically and are dependent on their environment which engages them and creates an atmosphere that feels comfortable to them. Yet they remain reliant on contact with another person.[2] Without someone to make contact with, without an opportunity to respond and without the care of another person, they would fall silent and lapse into physical inaction. If we reduce this illness to what is lost, we have not actually understood it. As heavy as these losses may weigh upon us and as easy as it is

[2] Andreas Kruse: *Lebensqualität bei Demenz? Zur Bewältigung einer Grenzsituation menschlichen Lebens.* (Heidelberg: Akademische Verlagsgesellschaft 2010).

to despair at them, they do not tell the true story of this illness. People with dementia not only live as its »bearer« but first and foremost as people with feelings that they sense and express, as people who are still dependent on relationships with other people, even if they may now appear in a different form. They are, in fact, fundamentally new relationships which must be developed.

They also are people who cannot continue to live without care, affection and appreciation. Their relationship to others and their being defined by such relationships also permeate their life, albeit a life which is now shaped by dementia. Though there may be inconsistency in the behavioural modes of dementia patients, in the most fundamental needs of human affinity they remain people just like everyone else. The continuity in relating to others is arguably the most remarkable experience that can be had with these patients because they show healthy people what is truly important in life: the feeling of emotional security. They long for a place to be, a gesture, or a person who can convey the feeling of emotional security, and this emotional security is not conceivable or palpable without true care and understanding.

The bodily self

When this feeling of emotional security is bestowed by means of a glance, an embrace or a gesture, it is possible to discover new and valuable sides to these people, as well as the numerous capabilities they still have. We discover how attentive dementia patients can be, how closely they can observe things and how they see and acknowledge things that are barely apparent to healthy people. They show us a new way of looking at the world because they can see the world in an unobstructed way and develop a feeling for subtle nuances in the tone of voice, in posture, in visual expression and in a handshake; nuances in everything which can be sensually grasped. Yet at the same time they demonstrate an ability for emotional warmth. Patients with dementia can be so kind, so naturally happy and so delighted with the smallest thing. In short, they are people who are unbelievably alive. They have a life which must be aroused by impulses, but it remains, nevertheless, a life full of intense experiences. As I have argued, at the beginning of the illness there is great despair, fear and shame. However, as the illness develops, this shame, and also the fear of the future, disappear, leaving a life which is lived in the here and now. Dementia patients very much depend on help and yet are alive from within; people living with dementia are still living *their* life; everyone enjoys their own things, has their own preferences, their own memories and their own individual way of expressing themselves. This has not changed.

Through their body patients with dementia continue to be someone very much alive. Physical experience imparts a kind of consciousness of presence. We need to challenge the idea that everything is controlled by the cerebrum. Without even having a reflexive relationship to my action, I can be aware of the physical expression of my feelings, that I exist, since a basic level of me remains in them. In this context, the philosopher of the body Hermann Schmitz speaks of the »corporeal I« which enables an affective relationship to oneself by means of corporeal feelings. When patients with dementia experience anger because the other person does not understand their concern, or when they start to cry because they feel helpless, these physical expressions can only be interpreted as manifestations of one's own self and thus as a pre-reflexive form of experience of the self.

Identity founded on relationship

This brings us to the most important point. People with dementia do indeed lose continuity with their life history and the thread of their former biography. However, their biography in fact survives and is preserved. Their memories remain fragmentary and can no longer be embedded in their overall history, and yet they remain someone with their own independently evolved identity and with their own character. This identity must, however, be created through a relationship to them. One great tragedy for dementia patients is that the more loved ones give up on them and the more their surroundings stereotype their behaviour, the more access to their identity becomes impossible. They need people who do not simply reduce them to what they can no longer be, but instead who, through a lively relationship, give them the possibility to express their identity. After all, identity is not simply a fact to be determined, identity is a dynamic process. In order to attain their identity, dementia patients need contact with other people. They need someone who awakens in them the possibility of identity and who effectively creates identity by means of encouragement.

Such a partner speaks sensitively to dementia patients, does not correct them, and does not confront them with the reality of a healthy person, but rather offers them the chance to resonate with them by recognising the reality of a dementia patient as being a relevant reality for them and reacts to it and react to it. This helps patients to live out their own experiences and in doing so to get a sense of their own identity: identity in the here and now. Here and now patients discover their imagined reality as *theirs,* and in this experience of immanence they can become aware of their own self. At that moment when someone takes their reality seriously, shares it with them, and is with them, they feel alive. An encounter with someone else plays a constructive role here, for it brings about a new feeling, the feeling of being someone. Whether patients with dementia can experience themselves as someone like that is not dependent on the symptoms of their illness, but solely on how intensively and sincerely we show them attentive care and show interest in the other person's desire to discover; someone who has indeed changed, but in their innermost core remains deeply connected to the healthy person and will always remain such. In this way, when the healthy person addresses and communicates with them that the people who are ill get their identity back, not by addressing them as someone who has dementia but as a person.

It is a great gift to be able to communicate with a sick person, not only for them, but also and perhaps even more so for the healthy person; for they are the creators, who, by being interested in the patient, strike a chord which no-one believed was still there. As long as this life continues there are surprises, provided one is prepared for the signals which dementia patients, in their own particular way, send out, provided one learns how to interpret those signals, and provided one is prepared to go along a shared path with the patient, a path that in the end will change both parties.

It is certainly not possible to simply ignore the tragic side of the illness. The tragedy of dementia cannot and should not be played down. However, a life with people suffering from dementia need not result in monotonous nursing. It can be something lively every time. There will not be a reliable continuity to it: liveliness will constantly come to life and die down, but it will come to life again. One simply has to want to discover the signs of life. In this case, life with a father, uncle or friend suffering from dementia, or with a sick wife, grandmother or sister will remain an animated life, troublesome and painful, but at the same time animated, sometimes even humorous, innocent, and natural. A full life in these small moments which emanate from the special ability of these people to feel relationships and to experience interpersonal contact. Thus, a full life is not achieved automatically. It is first generated by working on relationships. It is a task which is both pleasant and rewarding, as the healthy person quickly learns along with the patient how to delight in small things and to experience these small things to the full, to absorb them as an elixir of life. Patients with dementia need our help, but in receiving this they give us a lot back. They help us to realise that being human means more than what we are in our strongest years.

Anyone who really gets involved in dealing with dementia patients can learn from them that our life as a healthy person is frequently fixed in one direction, on reason, performance, functionality and productivity. They cut through this image of the human being and show us that we are deceiving ourselves in this idea of humanity geared towards performance, and that being human is richer and more diverse than we had originally believed.

They show us that every person has feelings hidden inside them which sometimes do not assert themselves over an entire lifetime. In healthy people these feelings – in a similar way to a dementia patient's memory – are buried beneath a one-sided idea of what a good life entails. They are buried by conforming to what is perceived to be expected of a person in order to be socially recognised. Patients with dementia ignore all these tendencies towards social conformity and open our eyes to a socially unrestricted view of the world. They do not show us anything that would be alien to us, but instead transport us to all the emotional levels of life that all humans have within them, but which, as rationally oriented healthy individuals, we all too often allow to wither away.

People suffering from dementia are people very much alive, who have much to offer. They have the power to put our view of humanity into perspective and to remind us that we do not become human beings through our intelligence and the cognitive synopsis of our life history. Our body can also tell such a story, as we also draw on earlier experiences via our physical access to the world. In this way, dementia patients correct our one-sided cognitive image of humanity and remind us that sense, feeling and intuition are as important as reason. Schopenhauer sums this up perfectly in his major work *The World as Will and Presentation* when he writes: »The human being is in his heart not in his head.«

We can thank dementia patients for one more thing. Their existence makes it strikingly clear that we live in a society where we have to relearn concern for others. The tragedy of dementia not only lies in the sad fact that this disease exists, it also lies in the fact that our society has forgotten how to keep weak and dependent people in our midst. Many people find dementia patients unsettling because they point out to us how, until now, we have failed in our efforts to fully integrate the weak into our social community. Perhaps this ability, which we have lost, to place these dependent people at the centre of our society is more tragic than the illness itself, since this tragedy could be mitigated through community. Thus, the challenge of dementia can also be viewed as an opportunity for a new approach to rediscovering care for the weak as a central cultural achievement of humanity.

This inability of the modern world to place vulnerable people at the centre of society, not through a sense of repugnance, but through a sense of deep appreciation, connects dementia with our last topic concerned with practical medicine, the subject of dying.

4. The dying person: When caring becomes the purpose of life

> »It is as if we did not know all of life if we do not, in a sense, include death in the circle.«
>
> *Wilhelm von Humboldt*

In a talk show a young lady spoke about how her father had taken his own life due to an incurable illness and the programme host wanted to know if I, as an ethicist, would view this suicide as a suicide by choice. It annoyed me that we have forgotten how to react adequately to suicide. In the case of suicide, why do we ask about the freedom of choice and not about the distress behind it? How can a situation arise where we think a suicide would be a good solution, as long as it is voluntary? A person prefers not to be in our midst and we assert: »If the person wants to do that in an enlightened way then that's all right!« As this television programme pointed out to me, apparently the moral challenge simply consists in making sure that this step is sufficiently well-considered. In my view, that is a reductionist approach to this vitally important topic and is, at the same time, ethical resignation.

We live in an age where we believe that wanting to continue to live is no longer self-evident and that it is ultimately up to the individual whether he or she wants to go on living or not. Prolonging life has, therefore, become an option which we are free to choose and in which no-one is allowed to interfere: A society of individual beings who live just for themselves and who should die for themselves. Tacitly, we have said goodbye to the idea of living in a community and believe that all the problems of modern man and woman, even the most critical ones, are solely to be determined by individual conviction and have nothing to do with the society in which the individual lives. In fact, we are taking less and less into account that what individuals want and what they freely choose are connected to the community in which they live. In fact, more than that: we are increasingly suppressing the idea that the individual would be altogether incapable of making decisions, even existing at all without a community.

This is also the case with suicide. We simply ask whether the individual has acted in a well-considered way. By asking this question we are rationalising suicide and turning it into a question of clever choice, making it the result of a rational calculation, as if life were a financial stock whose value we check every day in order to decide if we should keep it or offload it before it falls further in value. Everyone is to recalculate their »biocapital« on a daily basis and decide entirely independently if they would like to continue living or not. Hence, life is a case of balancing the pros and cons and making the decision to weigh up the result at the end. Depending on this outcome, we opt to either prolong life or not. This corresponds with an economic pattern of thought which, to all intents and purposes, has become socially acceptable. The fact that there is a tragic life behind the decision to not want to live any longer is concealed by the tendency to make suicide entirely plausible.

When I talk about tragedy here, as the term suggests, I am saying that we do not do justice to the human being by reverting to a moralisation of suicide. It is not for us to give a moral evaluation of suicide. As much as historical thinking may have tackled this issue, it cannot here be a matter of whether suicide as such is a good thing or a bad thing. As an ethicist, I am interested in the question of the distress these individuals feel, who even consider killing themselves. That is why I am speaking of tragedy.

This tragedy begins long before anyone even entertains the idea of suicide. It has already begun at the point where the idea develops in our consciousness that our life is only worth living for as long as we can do everything alone; on our own without the help of others. It already begins at the point where, in our healthiest years, we view the waning of strength, the possibility of becoming ill, old and infirm, as stages of decline in the human condition and believe that we recognise in this the beginnings of a loss of autonomy. Since we believe autonomy means being able to do things without the help of a third party, we are gripped by the idea of only wanting to live for as long as we are autonomous, in the sense of being totally independent of others. The tragedy implicit in this way of thinking lies in the fundamental non-redeemability of this claim. For when we make this claim upon our life, we misjudge the fact that we are already dependent on others. Would it make any sense to articulate these thoughts about independence if these other people did not exist? Is it not primarily the existence of other people that actually gives meaning to my words and my thoughts about myself? Moreover, in the end, have I not received everything that makes me who I am from others? The language that I speak is the result of the culture which had already existed without me. It is the result of the intentional care afforded me by others. The fact that I am psychologically healthy at all is due to people who, by their care, have made this health possible. Without them I would not only not be healthy, I would not be here at all. It is other people who have made it possible and continue to make it possible for me to exist – and now I think I can only lead a good life if I lead it completely detached from others.

Autonomy as a creative interaction with dependence

We live in an age where we say people should be able to decide for themselves whether they would like to continue living or not. We have such a one-sided view of autonomy that we believe we can only be autonomous when we manage entirely without the help of others.

With this understanding we inevitably devalue all dispensable life and reject all forms of life that require the help of another person. We no longer reflect on the fact that we are dependent on others throughout our life. This is replaced by the illusion of control over life until death.

The basis for this conception is the idea that being dependent on others would be the same as losing one's autonomy. This equation is untenable in this apodictic form. Anyone who gives the matter more careful consideration must recognise that autonomy cannot mean being able to do everything without the help of a third party. For in this case, not one single person would be truly autonomous. On the contrary, autonomy has much more to do with dealing with the unavoidable relationships of dependence in such a way that people can be themselves *through them.* The point is to learn creatively to rely on others every single day and in countless ways. Denying one's dependence basically constitutes self-deception: without other people we could not accomplish anything whatsoever. We are dependents all along; it is only the degree of dependence which changes with age. It is important to strengthen this connection between autonomy and dependence, in order to save people from despair.

With age, this dependence on other people's help becomes normal. We must find an accepting way of dealing with this, rather than pursuing total independence to no avail. It is worth putting into perspective the media's much vaunted ideal of a life shaped entirely by self-determination and instead pointing out people's resources in regard to their uncircumventable dependence. We can be free *in* dependence, for genuine concern is not patronising, but it rather addresses the uniqueness of people and attempts to emphasise their individuality. It makes it possible for them, step by step, to express themselves in their own individual manner. To be dependent does not mean the end of autonomy, but rather it is the condition for being able to live at all. However, for as long as this is understood to be a humiliation of being human, of being in a situation of existential dependence, suicide appears a logical conclusion. The problem is not the dependence itself, but rather the socially conditioned idea that human beings can only really be themselves in a state of self-assurance and autonomy.

People's fear of loss of control is widely prevalent today, more so than previously, and is distressing for many. The fear of being attached to machines at the end of their lives and the fear of the total loss of control and of helplessness leads some people contemplate premature suicide. Our society does not want to accept this fear and construes it as an emotional appeal for freedom and autonomy, but this pathos is one which, in the end, leaves the doubting and despairing individuals on their own. A humane society cannot be brought about through freedom alone if this freedom is not embedded in a culture of solidarity with the (ostensibly) weakest.

A seriously ill person also has potential

It must, therefore, be the objective of medical practice to do everything it can to ensure that situations do not arise where sick people feel stripped of their freedom and feel helpless.

Medical practice which places its trust in the omnipotence of machines and purely functional thinking, which treats laboratory results rather than seeing the people behind the results, this type of medical practice arouses fear and drives many people to a form of preventative suicide. Against this background, the solution offered by medical practice cannot just be the noncommittal offer of assisted suicide. It should, instead, be a solution which assuages people's fears by making them aware that medical practice is based on care and not on machinery. Rather than bringing the option of »free« suicide into play, medical practice should do everything to make it clear that even at the moment and from the moment of illness, the chances of leading an autonomous or self-determined life are in no way lost. From the perspective of the strong and healthy years of our life we cannot even imagine how much our view of life will change – the kinds of appreciation, attention, and surrender to the moment we can master – if or when the scope of our sovereignty over our lives narrows through age or illness (see chapter 2). From the very moment of becoming ill, we think that everything is over, without seeing that, even in sickness, we are still ourselves, that we retain our personality and that we can lead our life with a creative approach to our illness. The role of medical practice should be to point out how much potential even a sick person has. Medical practice must realise that its fundamental mission lies in promoting the development of each individual's potential. Medical care is about caring for others. And at the heart of this care and concern for others is the ability to enable those who are ill to be themselves.

A Lack of Belief in the Solidarity of Others

At this point, we can see how one-sided discussions are that are solely limited to the question of establishing whether the desire for suicide was »well-considered«. Care and concern is clearly seen here to be of secondary importance, although it should be the first consideration in the question of assisted suicide. For the decision to kill oneself, or the desire to be assisted by a doctor to do so, does not simply emanate from an inner personality. It must also be seen as a reaction to, and a reflection of, the signals a person receives from society. People do not decide by themselves what their path should be. They choose this path as a result of what is communicated to them by their environment. Consider the case of footballer Timo Konietzka who killed himself because he said he did not want to be a burden on others. Here we have the anticipation or the fear of a disunited society which took away his courage to face life.

This is precisely the dangerous point in discussions about assisted suicide. When we think that it would be the most humane thing to fulfil the wish of any person to commit suicide, if he or she really wanted to, we are suggesting that, in certain cases, it would be sensible not to want to live any longer. By doing this we are trivialising death, which is highly problematic. In my view, self-chosen death cannot simply be accepted as normal. It cannot be perceived as normality because, ultimately, it refers to interpersonal contexts which led to the wish arising in the first place.

The socially acknowledged worthlessness of life

Now, it could be argued that everyone should be able to decide for themselves whether they would like to go or to stay. Indeed any form of patronisation is totally unacceptable here. There can be no question of wanting to know better what is good for others; it is always necessary to respect the uniqueness of a person and to make this the basis for everything. Therefore, it must be recognised that the reasons for suicide can be extremely diverse and not all fit in with the explanation which I have just developed. Yet it would be an ethical resignation if we were to simply accept the wish to prefer to die rather than to live and were to accept it as being unalterable and even destined. In the case of life and death, it seems to me that we should not accept any kind of adverse situation in society. Who says that nothing can be done against the circumstances in society? Even though it might be »sensible« to prefer death in the face of imminent fear; what is this fear when it concerns illness, infirmity and assisted suicide? Is it not the fear of being a worthless person who simply drops out of a society composed of the strong? But what if society were to rethink this and turn its values upside down, as for example the hospice services do when they relay to those dying how much they receive from them and in fact how much *these* people in particular can give back to their helpers? Whether someone wishes to die or continue living in the face of illness does not depend solely on the kind of society in which people consider themselves to be, although it is unquestionably important. It depends on the social framework and on an expectancy of what other people think about people when they are seriously and incurably ill. When we regard taking the path of assisted suicide as a medical service, as one choice among others, we simply accept too readily that there are people in our society who do not believe in the solidarity of their fellow men and women, who as seriously ill people do not feel valued, but rather devalued because they are now »only« lying in bed. This needs to be reconsidered.

Conveying affirmation of life as an uncircumventable task of society

An experience during a panel discussion has stayed with me for quite some time. It concerned a self-assured author in the panel discussion who vehemently argued that, should his circumstances demand it, he would have to be granted the right to assisted suicide, as was his entitlement as a free person to decide whether he wished to continue living or not. After he had made his case, a young woman in the audience stood up and asked him: »You just said you had four children. If I were your daughter and were I to ask you to rethink your wish to kill yourself, and asked you not to do it, would you still want to commit suicide?« The man was visibly affected by this question and replied with little hesitation or deliberation: »In that case, of course not ...« The young woman's question had obviously given him much to think about. This also stayed with me for a long time; for if the appeal of a daughter could have such a positive effect why could this not be evoked by a doctor, a carer or even a fellow human being?

This particular experience points out once again (particularly in view of the author's original resolve) that the desire to commit suicide is indeed the result of different experiences and not simply a logical calculation. It is our experience with other human beings which gives rise to such wishes and it is the lack of experience of solidarity, of interpersonal care and of being unconditionally loved, which drives people to suicide.

We talk so much about freedom, deliberation and formalistic implications, but the most important aspect is the question of whether a person is still loved. What matters is the question of whether we live in a society in which people who are ill are actually perceived to be valuable human beings. What matters is whether we succeed in bringing forward a culture of care in which the seriously ill person does not feel undervalued, but instead can experience a new sense of meaning through the care of fellow human beings and a form of medical practice that places respect and relationships centre stage. If, however, even doctors talk about »untreatable patients« or »hopeless cases«, they are suggesting that these people have forfeited every chance of being perceived as human beings for whom we struggle and fight, for whom we go out of our way, for whom we step into the breach and for whom nothing is too much trouble. Many people fear that they, being in need of care, simply represent an imposition on their fellow human beings, who have better things to do than look after worthless sick people.

Assisted suicide as an implicit abrogation of duty by society

Once assisted suicide has been propagated as a recognised solution, it appears more sensible for a society to follow this path than to fight for people, to stand up for their will to live, and to ensure that a fundamental affirmation of life, based on mutual dependency, becomes an essential aim of society. This is the underlying problem of assisted suicide. The desire to continue to live will eventually no longer be seen as the most natural thing, but rather only as an option, as the result of a personal choice, which one »reasonably« could have made differently. Ultimately, this conveys the idea that in certain cases one may have forfeited one's right to assistance by a third party, since there are cases in which it appears reasonable not to live any longer. All at once, people affected will have to justify why, in spite of chronic pain, they prefer to continue living, even preferring to go on living when they impose a duty on their fellow human beings to care for and support them. In this case, freedom can even mean: You can always kill yourself if you don't feel well! When they do not feel well and do not kill themselves, but instead hope to receive support, the feeling gradually creeps in that they must somehow provide justification for this desired help. Some people who ended their lives simply lost heart in believing in the implicitness of support. Therein lies the real tragedy of endorsing assisted suicide as a solution for the suffering of people who are ill. Making medical assistance a service of choice means relieving society of its duty to support sick people from isolation, devaluation, and despair. The more assisted suicide is promoted as a normal and acceptable alternative to life, the more care appears as one option among others for isolated and seriously ill people, and even to a certain extent as an unnecessary one, since suicide offers a less troublesome alternative. It seems important to me, particularly nowadays, to opt for a commitment against despair and instead to seek more capacity for hope.

In other words, the approval of suicide would amount to a limitation of society's efforts to do everything imaginable to prevent such suicidal wishes even arising. Ultimately, the normalisation of assisted suicide resembles a conscious calculation of a situation that can never actually be »normal«, but instead always remains tragic. This tragedy is trivialised if we introduce assistance for suicide as a service provision of choice. Suicide remains an open wound, which is not healed by the fact that it takes place autonomously. And because it remains an open wound, the answer to the desire to commit suicide can only be a radical momentum towards elimination of the reasons for suicide, and not the operational normalisation of a tragic action.

Privatisation of a social deficiency

The normalisation of assisted suicide would be a further step towards a privatisation of hopelessness, which closes its eyes to the fact that a person's despair inevitably has a social and macrosocial component. We act as though the desire to commit suicide or not depends on individual preference, which signifies making the individual the initiator of the necessity of suicide. By doing so we overlook the fact that internalised social conceptions are reflected in an individual's desire. The fact that people feel worthless, burdensome and even an imposition on others cannot simply be perceived as a preference, but rather should be seen as an expression of adverse social circumstances and at the same time as an internalisation of macrosocial conceptions that cannot simply be ignored. I am talking about a collective interpretative conception according to which there is life that is not worth living. We live in a society where precisely this message is implicitly being conveyed: we can lose the value of our life at any time, whether through illness, disability, or self-denial. This relates to the apparent consensus that life itself is not of value, rather only when it achieves something. People threatened by illness have internalised this social consensus and use it as motivation for their own preferences. When we now react to the internalisation of this socially conveyed attitude by stating that the sick, the old and other people who feel that they are of no value could just take leave of us of their own accord, we are making this attitude socially acceptable, and in so doing we are failing to send a strong signal that we oppose it.

The number one priority of society lies in asking if we have really done everything we can to relieve the distress of people wanting to die. Have we done everything we can to alleviate their intolerable pain? What have we possibly missed when they consider their suffering to be too great? We have to ask ourselves whether we have sufficiently made it clear to people wishing to die that they can still be themselves, even if they are more heavily dependent on others at the end of their life than before. We must grant them this space for reflection and our support as a matter of course, as something which no person needs to justify. To view a person's suffering simply as a task of organising to kill them or of organising their suicide is short-sighted. If they are so desperate that they would rather die, then in fact we have to do our utmost to point out new possibilities, however small they might be.

Another experience also made me think. It concerned a book[1] I had been asked to review for a well-known magazine, a book which strongly advocated a normalisation of assisted suicide and which had received excellent reviews in all journals. I thought it could be a good opportunity to learn something new and so I began to read the book. But the more I read, the more I asked myself why it was so highly praised. Obviously, it expressed popular opinion, but the book spurred me on to question the theme more closely. In the book, the author proposes, sincerely and with the air of objectivity, that we divide suicidal wishes into reasonable and unreasonable wishes. To do this, he recommends questioning whether the suicidal wish of a patient satisfies »rational cri-

[1] Uwe-Christian Arnold, *Letzte Hilfe. Ein Plädoyer für das selbstbestimmte Sterben.* (Hamburg: Rowohlt 2014).

teria« or not. He goes on to explain what he understands as reasonable: »Mr D. had lived his life, but from now on he could no longer expect an improvement in his living situation. In fact, just the opposite: he was completely bed-ridden and in need of care«[2]. According to the author, it was a rational decision for Mr D. to want to kill himself. The book is dedicated to the promotion of a particular vision of a life worth living, which, naturally, can be held by an individual, but which cannot be construed as a model of reasonableness. The fact that the author can, nevertheless, construe such an illegitimate generalisation without a single reader challenging it, made me realise how natural it has become to view a life dependent on care as a life which can be rejected. That is the tragedy which I associate with the wide acceptance of such a book. Remarkably, the author differentiates between people who take their lives for »wrong« reasons at the wrong time from those who do it at the »right« time and for the right reasons.[3] According to the author, people with the wrong reasons »were in need of good psychological support, solid assistance to live and *not* assistance to commit suicide«.[4] The others, by contrast, were in need of good support and assistance *for* suicide. Suicide after a stroke or even suicide linked to old age are stated, in principal, to be rational acts without any kind of protest to the contrary, which shows how deeply rooted our collective negative evaluation of an invalid's life has become.

If we follow this to its logical conclusion we are suggesting that it would be almost irrational not to hope for assistance to commit suicide, but instead support for living, when »bedridden and dependent on care«. I find it deeply depres-

[2] Ibid., p. 58.
[3] Ibid., p. 43 and p. 182.
[4] Ibid., p. 43.

sing to have to read in this book, which has certainly enjoyed widespread appeal: »Almost everyone of sound mind would choose to leave this life quickly and painlessly rather than spending two or three weeks in the process of dying, where one is heavily dependent on the help of others.«[5]

The author states that the desire of a patient in need of care to commit suicide is an »understandable, consistent or inevitable reaction to particular circumstances of life«.[6] Consequently, this means that whoever is dependent on care and does not want to kill him or herself is actually inconsequent. Inevitably, this means that the desire for suicide automatically arises in care dependency and there is no means of supporting people *in* their dependency and giving them back their quality of life. So where are, at the very least, the entitlement to, and the commitment to, comfort and the improvement of care in the final stages of life? According to Arnold, it would be »unreasonable to want to prevent suicide *per se*. We should, of course, reduce the appallingly high rate of suicides brought on by despair [...], but certainly not the relatively small number of cases where people deliberately choose a well-considered suicide.«[7]

Thus, in the author's opinion, we should »in no way« take steps to improve the situation of these people! Even the attempt to reduce »carefully considered suicide« seems inappropriate to him.

I have used excerpts from this book here, because it has opened my eyes. It has shown me that we are living in an age where people no longer dare to hope; to hope that it is a matter of course that they will be cared for when they are old or become seriously ill. People clearly no longer believe that

5 Ibid., p. 38.
6 Ibid., p. 182.
7 Ibid.

even »stroke patients« can cast off the feeling of having become completely worthless, if they are cared for by doctors and carers. Since they no longer believe or dare to dream for a moment of support in their time of infirmity, many people consider it to be »sensible« or »reasonable« to end their lives prematurely. I believe that such a situation is simply = unacceptable.

Against the background of a rhetoric of plausibility which we are constantly exposed to these days, and with regard to the pervasive and vociferous pleas for a normalisation of assisted suicide, it is important to make it clear that, initially, the underlying reason for a desire to commit suicide is nothing more than ambivalence. The desire to die is not simply something which cannot be circumvented but rather is a fluctuating desire, a situation of being torn between wanting to live and not being able to bear it any longer. From the desire to kill oneself it is usually understood that people affected believe their situation is futile, hopeless and inescapable. And from their position of a loss of future prospect, the idea of continuing to live is worse than dying. But this does not mean that people primarily wish to die, instead they desire different circumstances for living, which seem, however, unattainable. If we choose assisted suicide as an effective solution, and as a result of this feeling of oppression, we have ultimately given up and leave the patients situation just as it is, since their departure from life seems the obvious path.

In other words, we need easy access to professional support for suicidal people so that they can be helped as early as possible. People who would rather die than go on living need to have, first and foremost, the feeling that they can discuss the situation with their doctors. One of the major concerns of the present situation is that patients are often reluctant to talk about their suicidal thoughts because many of them fear they will end up in a psychiatric ward. This is an extremely dangerous and negative situation because we are abandoning them in their distress and need. We need a more open discussion on thoughts about suicide, for only then will we create opportunities to provide expert help to those who are worn down with despair.

Towards a culture of recognition and reintegration of the critically ill into society

People who are distressed because of their illness and frailty must know that they can always choose freely and that nobody will defy their wishes. They have to be assured that they will never be ignored or have to do anything against their will. They have to have the confidence to know that they can, at any time, be spared a purely technical but pointless treatment and will never be denied the right to refuse a course of action. The most basic principle of an ethics of care is to make others the focal point and not one's own particular view. Yet in view of the position of weakness in which people willing to die find themselves, simply granting this freedom cannot be enough. Instead, it is a matter of recognising the other person as someone who is intrinsically valuable, who can never lose his or her dignity, regardless of the situation. Respecting this dignity means giving the patients the feeling, in every situation, that they are special. The objective must, therefore, be to do everything humanly possible to bring suicidal people, who inevitably find themselves in a position of extreme loneliness, back into the community, a community which reintegrates them.

The key role of medical practice and society is, in short, to send a signal to people who are worried about their infirmity that they do not have to accomplish anything to be recognised as valued people. It is essential to counter the isolation of a lot of sick people and to give their lives new meaning in such a way that they do not see themselves as »a problem to be treated«, and which creates work for others. On the contrary, they must be allowed to realise that society is grateful to have them in its midst and the whole of society must convey to people who are ill that they have much to give back to society.

The reassurance of unconditional acceptance by others, as long as this is a collective agreement, can give rise to something like comfort, relief, perhaps hope, even the feeling of heart-felt support by others. This comfort and hope can only be felt if one is surrounded by people who send out the right signals. Signals which make it clear that people who are struggling with infirmity will not be left on their own by their fellow human beings and indeed by the whole of society. This message can only be conveyed by the establishment of a new culture in dealing with chronically ill people; through the establishment of a culture, which makes it clear that even a person in the greatest need of care has much to give us, simply by being a human being.

It is becoming increasingly important in our times not to lose sight of the fact that the role of humane medicinal practice cannot be understood to be dealing only with correct procedure or the completion of a duty. Appropriate action and fulfilment of duty are essential prerequisites for good medical practice, but these two factors alone do not make medical practice humane or compassionate. More must be invested in interhuman relationships in medical treatment and everything must be done to ensure that the sick and frail are not pushed to the margins, but instead are placed at the centre of our deeply rationalised daily lives. Ultimately, we will have to recognise that even the best organised medical practice only becomes humane medical practice if good organisation is integrated into personal care, which must be taken as a given, and which, even in times of weakness, gains a value which no society can do without.

We have now identified the practical relevance of four highly significant issues in modern medicinal practice and attempted to develop a small phenomenology of people who are ill. By doing this, we have placed the focus on people themselves, their mental state, their existential threat and their world. It is a focus which has almost been forgotten in modern medical practice, a practice that is heavily oriented towards pragmatism. Based on these practical examples, it is now a question of determining key values that need to be considered if we want to help seriously ill people with the existential challenges that come with illness, so that they are in a position to retain their own distinctive personality in spite of their illness. In order to achieve this, I have singled out four aspects I consider innovative and forward-looking: learning to accept, trust, hope and – the basis for all three – understanding. Whilst the first three values relate to sick people and thus are meant to help them find their own way, to contend with themselves and the outside world, understanding represents the enabling condition the other three are geared towards. In other words, only when doctors, psychotherapists and carers *understand* the existential distress of sick people will it be possible for sick people to open themselves up to the idea of acceptance, trust and hope. In this respect, Chapter Four constitutes both the foundation and the ramifications resulting from the previous three chapters.

We will begin with learning to accept. In order to learn to accept our life as it is, it is important first of all to think about »destiny«, not in the sense of a hypostasised power of destiny, but rather to the effect that we all are born into a particular world and that this world must inevitably be seen as part of our destiny. Only when we recognise the world as it is, will we be in a position to accept things (such as illness), even if we never chose them.

III.
Paths to Coping and Overcoming

5. Learning to accept: The good life as the art of reestablishing ourselves

»The human being is the being that is condemned to transform necessity into freedom.«

José Ortega y Gasset

The Austrian author Marie von Ebner-Eschenbach expressed it succinctly when she wrote, »It is not what we experience, but how we feel about what we experience that shapes our destiny«. This is something we all too easily forget in our world characterised by technology and practicality. These days, it is, admittedly, not easy to speak about destiny, for destiny appears to be something modern man should actually have consigned to history. Its inflated use in various twentieth-century ideologies has led to its widespread discreditation. Certainly in philosophy, Jürgen Habermas considered it plausible to maintain that, as an expression of a regression into non-conceptual and mythical thinking, »destiny« had finally served its purpose.[1] Today, destiny is, above all, perceived as being something that should not exist since we associate with it the feeling of helplessness, threat and relentlessness. Yet the term destiny is ambiguous. It is important to address it today because this analysis can help us adopt an attitude to life which proves to us that we are not simply at the mercy of destiny.

What is the actual meaning of the word destiny? The earliest associations are connected with the power of destiny,

[1] Jürgen Habermas, *Vorstudien und Ergänzungen zu einer Theorie des kommunikativen Handelns* (Frankfurt am Main: Suhrkamp 1984), p. 489.

Moira. The idea of destiny as the result of impersonal power was first described in the Homeric epics. Significant characteristics of this accepted power of destiny are its arbitrariness and unpredictability. It defies rational comprehension and we therefore still speak today of blind destiny, about its »moods«, about destiny that knows no laws, no reason and no logic. This concept of the power of destiny is encapsulated in the metaphor of the threads of destiny, which are spun by the three Moirai: destiny in the hands of Lachesis is related to the past, Klotho is related to the present and Atropos to the future. Atropos is undoubtedly the best known figure, as she cuts the thread of destiny and thus represents a person's death.

What does destiny mean?

Whilst destiny in its earliest conception was viewed as absurd and incomprehensible, the Stoics developed a completely different understanding of destiny, which has become known as fate, embodied in Heimarmene, the goddess of fate. Stoic thinkers interpret fate not as an impersonal and arbitrary power of destiny, but rather the opposite, as the well-orderedness of the world and as an event in the world driven by logos. Their view of the world was of an all-embracing providence and order which systematically controlled everything in the world.

Linked to this concept is the idea of predetermination or cosmological determinism; to explain the course of events, the Stoics speak of a causal chain (this is the origin of the term »Heimarmene«, which approximates to »series of causes«). Yet it would be too simple to understand this causal chain in a way that leaves no room for the freedom of humans. The Stoics placed an emphasis on human freedom, for, according to them, whilst events in the world do follow a causal chain, people are free either to submit to the natural law within it or overcome it through their own inner will. Even though today we still understand a fatalist to be someone who views things as inevitable and thus accepts the course of events without resistance, the idea of inner human freedom was already addressed in Ancient Rome, for example in Cicero's book *On Fate* dating from 44 BC. Even at that time the relationship between freedom and destiny/fate or between a more deterministic worldview and the idea that human will was not completely determined by natural laws were being discussed. We can see this in the work of one of Aristotle's students, Alexander of Aphrodisias, dating from 200 AD: »Belief in fate is abdicating responsibility and not a philosophical approach. Fate is the same as nature. As humans can act against nature they can also act against fate. Whoever denies the ability to choose by reason as a principle of action, negates mankind itself.«[2] Increasingly in Late Antiquity the idea gained acceptance that the course of the world is shaped by fate, but that not everything occurs with absolute necessity, because people are free in their action. By their actions they can initiate causes, which do not change the world as a whole but change how things evolve and their influence on the world.

Besides the power of fate in Greek mythology and the cosmic ordering of fate of the Stoics, a third meaning of fate or destiny can be identified: fate as something which befalls us and is contingent. Niklas Luhmann defines contingency as

---

[2] Cited according to Markus Enders, »Das Schicksal in der Antike und seine Bedeutung für das Machbarkeitsdenken heute«. In: Imago Hominis. *Quartalschrift für Medizinische Anthropologie und Bioethik* no. 18, vol. 2 (2011), pp. 121–136.

that which »is neither *necessary* nor *impossible*«.[3] It stands for the unpredictable, the unavailable and, at the same time, for that with which we must reckon at any given time. There are also old terms for this third meaning, such as the »Tyche«, where fate is referred to as something which occurs but could not have been predicted and for which there does not need to have been a higher controlling power. This is linked to an understanding of the irrefutability of fate. What occurs might not actually have occurred (contingency), however, it *is* here now. Fate is always a fact, a fact which affects me, concerns me and shocks me. It is something which is irresolvable, regardless of whether one recognises its necessity or not. The philosopher of religion Romano Guardini summed it up: »The world did not have to be the world it is; it is now that world, it is now immutable«.[4] It certainly need not remain immutable, for we have the ability to act, but only if we recognise the factuality of what it is. I consider this third meaning of fate to be crucial: the recognition that there is something which is inaccessible and which people cannot decide on. This third concept of fate signifies nothing less than a fundamental indeterminateness of reality. Indeterminate, because firstly there is an inaccessible core in everything which an individual cannot influence, secondly because a course of events cannot be completely planned and thus remains unpredictable, and thirdly because there are unforeseen events which can occur at any time, but might not. When we speak of what we experience and of fate, we also mean precisely this aspect of wavering between what is possible, but not necessary. Fate befalls us without recognisable context. It descends

---

[3] Niklas Luhmann, *Soziale Systeme. Grundriss einer allgemeinen Theorie* (Frankfurt am Main: Suhrkamp 1987), p. 152.

[4] Romano Guardini, *Freiheit, Gnade, Schicksal* (Mainz: Matthias-Grünewald-Verlag 1994), p. 160.

upon us as something inexplicable and presents a great challenge to our understanding of existence, which is accompanied by the need to resist doubt regarding the meaning »of it all«. The unpredictable impact of fate demonstrates to people how alien the world is and gives rise to a feeling of arbitrariness and helplessness.

The human being necessarily discovers what is already there

By virtue of these preliminary considerations it has already become clear that »fate« is an iridescent term. On the one hand, it is indispensable, and on the other, it is totally alien; for the purpose of fate is often not revealed and so initially gives rise to the feeling of absurdity. We should consider this third aspect of fate in more detail – the absolutely predetermined. Predetermined can have three meanings: (1) predetermined in the sense of the existing world, (2) predetermined in the sense of an event that was not chosen, a catastrophe, or (3) predetermined in the sense of an unpredictability of the consequences of one's own actions. Let us look at the first point.

The space and time of our existence is irrevocably predetermined; we are born somewhere and at some time, and this here and now of being born is something we do not do ourselves. Being born at one time and not another is part of our fate, for which we can blame no-one else. It is up to us to act on this predetermination. The same is true of the circumstances into which we are born. We have neither affected them nor were we able to choose them. In addition, we are born with particular characteristics, shortcomings and talents. These faculties we were given were also not chosen by us. They are simply there. Recognising this is the first prerequisite for being able to adequately deal with them.

It has become clear that the predetermination of one's own existence is not the same as the randomness or unintentionality of these precepts. Someone arriving in the world in some place or other is always dependent on other people having made a decision. Fate does not just appear from nowhere but is itself linked to numerous coincidences and prior decisions, which preceded the event of my birth and indeed are the prerequisites for my existence. A tiny coincidence or a change of plans at the last moment by one of my ancestors and I would not exist. But if a crucial aspect of fate is that people have no influence on it, then this definition says nothing about the reasons for these precepts and preconditions. Whatever other people do and affect will also ultimately play a part in my own fate.

We experience our own existential conditions as fundamentally inaccessible and not a matter of our choice. We did not make ourselves and have no influence on when we come, where we come to and above all whether we come at all. In this respect life itself is something that was not chosen and is inaccessible. The simple fact that we are here is the most powerful sign that we have more fate in us than we would sometimes like to admit.

Life means being exposed to what befalls us

Fate is, however, much more. Even when we are born and are now present, it is certainly not the case that we immediately step into the world and alter it through action. At first, we are less acting and more experiencing beings. Our life begins with our own experience of what happens to us. It begins with what we experience, without us in any way having chosen what it is we are experiencing. In fact, it can only happen to us *because* we could not choose it. Hence, we inevitably live in a mode experiencing. Human beings can do a lot, but they cannot do anything from nothing. Instead, they must set out from what is already given. The decision to do something is not simply a choice that results from nothing, but a result based on experience. They can, in fact, choose, but their choice is shaped by what they have experienced in their life. We often fail to recognise that we are always reacting, experiencing and being affected by what already exists. Strictly speaking we even have to accept that our thoughts are also a part of what is predetermined; they cannot be forced, they originate from a reason which is beyond our control. Both people's thoughts and actions are events based on inaccessible precepts.

We can understand our journey through life as an interplay between experience, which happens to us, and action, which we have actively seek. Every life is spent in this dialectic between action and experience, activity and sufferance, deciding and enduring things. There is no decision without endurance, because I would not know how to decide without the experience of something predetermined. It is this which shapes us and enables us to choose. It is not only the world which is predetermined; the actions of other people, with whom we are directly – and indirectly – connected, are also predetermined. Whether we like it or not, we are all a part of and dependent on the world of others. In the absence of this dependency, we would be unable to form relationships, interact with others and thus be unable to live. However, because we can never predict how other people will act, we remain in a mode of open development. Of course, we can actively step in, but again we become those who experience, because, with our actions, we trigger reactions which are never fully predictable. In short, we experience through action, and through experience we prepare new actions.

Being born can, therefore, be described as the true paradigm of human existence. People do not give birth to themselves, but rather they are born and are always and unavoidably born into an existing situation. They have to arrive here, search for their place, cultivate it and try to establish themselves. This process of self-establishment (which determines our life much more than »doing«) demands that I learn a basic approach to what I encounter, an attitude of acceptance without which I have no ties to any particular place. I have to learn to recognise the place I encounter as *my* place, as the place which above all else enables me to be »myself«. Recognising that without this place I would not exist represents the enabling condition for finding a way to develop within it. This was also the idea the Stoics had in mind (without expressing it in this way), when they spoke of the cosmos as logos and thereby recognising the world which surrounds me as well-ordered and intrinsically good. For this represents nothing less than the basic prerequisite for a successful and happy life. The main question for the Stoics was simply how human beings can be happy.

The modern inability to accept what is predetermined

Today, the place we find ourselves in is no longer an unquestionably valid place. Although we are outwardly better off than people in ancient times, the structure of the world that we have been born into has lost its comfort. Not because it has become more adverse than in ancient times, but because we look at it in a different light. We no longer perceive our world as ordered, as a reality that we can fundamentally accept. Instead, we believe the cosmos in which we live to be suboptimal, not quite good enough for us to feel totally secure and which we do not feel part of. We feel like strangers in an alien cosmos and are no longer a microcosm in a sovereign macrocosm. For this reason, we are no longer astounded by the all-encompassing order of the cosmos and the secret of our being, but rather we order our world with a view to the question of whether it could not be better than it is. Recently, Tom Knight, a research scientist from MIT in America, declared at a press conference: «The genetic code is 3.6 billion years old. It's time we wrote a new one.«[5] But that is not all: the biochemist Craig Venter said it was time to replace evolution with something better, namely a «second genesis«.[6] We no longer ask how we can fit into our world, but instead whether there is another, much better place. When I say »place« I do not mean a locality, it has more to do with the general pre-determinedness that we find in this world and at the same time in ourselves. So it is not uncommon we spend our whole lives searching for the perfect place and the perfect configuration of our being and do not risk settling down somewhere, constantly believing another better, even perfect place could turn up. We blame our unhappiness on the fact that fate did not grant us the right place to be, which has left us at a disadvantage since it put us in a place we did not want to be. Thus the simple conclusion is that we have no other option than to be unhappy in this »alien world«. Although we have never been able to choose our place in the world, people today still believe they should have the right to stack

---

5 Lee Silver, »Scientists push the boundaries of human life«. In: *Newsweek*, (2007) Internet Edition. Available online at: http://www.newsweek.com/id/34406 [Accessed 05. 07. 2015].

6 Cp. Craig Venter, »Second Genesis: Making new life«. In: *New Scientist*, (2009). Available online at: http://www.newscientist.com/article/mg20126990.200-second-genesis-making-new-life.html [Accessed 01. 07. 2015].

their own life-cards. Schopenhauer maintained precisely the opposite when he stated in his *Aphorisms on the Wisdom of Life*: »Fate shuffles the cards and we play«.[7] We play with the cards we have been dealt and we have every chance of playing well with them. We squander this opportunity, however, if we insist on sorting our hands ourselves, rather than simply taking the cards we are dealt. In other words, by doing this the game would already be decided, and what would life then be about? The profoundness of life comes about from the fact that we are brought into a world and faced with the task of becoming ourselves. The world makes us what we are. Jean Marolleau expresses this contingency perfectly in his book *Die Zukunftsgesellschaft* (*The Society of the Future*) when he writes: »For all their life, but particularly at the moment of their birth, human beings are subject to a chain of circumstances over which they have not the slightest influence and which contribute to their self-realisation by getting in their way materially.«[8]

Fate as a task

It is easy to overlook the fact that fate, in what it predetermines, is not fulfilling, is not the whole, but rather only a first step. It far from decides everything. The pre-determinateness of the world can ultimately be seen as a task to realise ourselves in correspondence with it and not as averse to it. In other words, it depends on the attitude with which we

[7] Arthur Schopenhauer, *Aphorismen zur Lebensweisheit* (Frankfurt am Main: Insel 1976), p. 198.

[8] Jean Marolleau, *Die Zukunftsgesellschaft*. Translated from French by P. Kamnitzer (Düsseldorf/Vienna: Econ-Verlag 1971), p. 114.

react to our existence in *this* world. Hermann Graf Keyserling once wrote: »Events in our lives are determined by what they mean to us«.[9] We are challenged to take responsibility for what is given to us and to shape it. Only through our attitude to this predetermined beginning will this beginning (and we ourselves) become actualised reality. Encountering fate presents us with a task and at the same time gives us the opportunity to fulfil this task.

In this context, illness is a good example. No-one chooses to become ill and no-one prefers illness to health. Instead, we should do everything we can to prevent illness. If illness does however strike, our fate is in no way sealed with its appearance. Illness is »fated«, but it does not conclude our fate. Nor does it seal the life of a person, but instead opens up, even to someone with an incurable illness, the possibility to relate to the illness in a way that corresponds with his or her inner personality. People who have become ill can also play with the cards they have been dealt, provided they become aware of this opportunity.

It is precisely at this juncture that medical practice has a great responsibility, as it is the principal point of contact for a sick person. If medical practice persists in its belief in pure practicability and in its tendency towards technological escalation, it will rob patients of the chance to recognise at least to a degree their illness as a part of their own biography. The more technology and procedures are promoted and the more illness is simply viewed as something disastrous against which the only reaction is to fight, the more sick people will be plunged into despair. They are supported in conquering their illness, but are ignored and uninformed that they have

---

[9] Hermann Keyserling, »Das Schicksals-Problem«. In: Hermann Keyserling, *Philosophie als Kunst* (Darmstadt: Otto Reichl 1922), pp. 145–161, p. 150.

within themselves the possibility to live their life even with the illness. Fate is not the final chord, but rather the prelude, the overture which opens up numerous opportunities for action.

The fate of a serious illness will always remain something to be resisted, something we have not willingly chosen for ourselves. It is and remains fateful. Yet its occurrence does not, at the same time, mean the end of a good life. How one experiences and lives with it depends a great deal on how one assimilates it (as something not wished for) and integrates it into one's own life story.

Freedom

These days we believe freedom can only exist when we finally begin at zero and can completely determine ourselves through ourselves. This is a mistake. Freedom does not exist where everything is freely available to us. Freedom requires the recognition of necessity. Kierkegaard put this succinctly in his book *The Sickness unto Death* when he talked of the »despair of possibility« and pointed to the necessity of the necessary. Fate is the compulsory necessity which we do not choose, but is required for people to be happy. It is the fact that there is fate in the sense of unsought for necessity which first produces our freedom: It is the challenge and not the absolute possibility by which man can feel free. A being with absolute freedom would be a being without fate. This absolute lack of fate is, however, not only illusory it is also not desirable, as it would rob us of every opportunity to be able to be and become ourselves. According to the theologist Paul Tillich, »all profound people suspect or know that their character, their self-given nature and also what seems external and random determine what affects them. Yet they know or suspect at the same time that their self-given nature, their character, is determined by events which go back to past generations, to past states of living substance and to past circumstances in the world. This means that necessity in terms of fate is necessity in being in general.«[10] Eliminating the challenges that the fateful conditions of our life place upon us, would not result in an increase in freedom, but instead mean a loss of our possibilities. If there were no challenges, no experiences, no striving for something, every freedom would be taken from us. A free person is not one who has unlimited access to all possibilities of action, but rather one who has learned to live, in a creative way, with what exists.

The fullness of life can only be experienced in the tension between fate and choice, between natural faculties and intellectual freedom and between calculable predictability and being fundamentally open to occurrences in the world. Calculability, predictability, proceduralisation and producing security are positive values of natural science. As a natural science, medicine assumes that a good laboratory result is necessarily a good result for people and for their understanding of themselves and this is precisely the grave misconception which we are taken in by. For here there is a basic misunderstanding that ignorance of, and unpredictability of, the course of people's life do not constitute a deficiency, but rather a blessing, because they can only make plans with a view to the inherent uncertainty of their future and so feel free in their planning. Planning, finalising and forecasting as values in themselves reduce human life to a functioning mechanism, which »runs its course« according to predetermined laws. However, planning in itself always signifies illegitimating

---

[10] Paul Tillich, »Philosophie und Schicksal«. In: *Kant-Studien 34* (1929), pp. 300–311, here p. 301 f.

life, which is defined by the fact that it withdraws from any predictability. With this withdrawal of the core elements of life, life will not increase in value, but will instead be radically devalued and forced into insignificance. It is important to look more closely at the value of an openness to life and not-knowing, at the mysterious character of all life and at the value of an open future.

What does all this mean for us today and for medicine? The fact that modern society and modern medical practice have become victims of a total suppression and denial of fate is linked to the fact that »values« shaped by technology and economisation increasingly permeate all areas of life in our society. In the context of this redefinition, we are ever more exclusively oriented towards processes, planning and controls. Our whole life is becoming a matter of management: what is unmanageable should not exist. In this manner of regimented thinking, fate becomes a bogeyman to be blindly eliminated. This attitude does not accept that what is predetermined, what exists unalterably, does not take a human being's freedom away, but rather enables freedom in the first place. This does not make the case for a new resignation to fate. Such an appeal would be inappropriate and unfair to human beings, endowed with intelligence. Our problematic handling of fate does not culminate in our idea of fighting fate; it culminates in the suggestion that modern man need not recognise or accept any form of fate whatsoever.

The Value of Self-Affirmation

As we have seen, fate can have several meanings. There is fate as necessity, without which the world would not exist, the fact that the world is here today simply as it is. Instead of lamenting the entirety of all fateful predeterminants, composure would be the right attitude; in the sense of Erich Frieds, »it is what it is«. Then there is fate as something adverse, which befalls the individual. It would be, without doubt, inappropriate to gloss over misfortunes and the tragedy associated with them, and here it would also be difficult to call for composure. Instead, it should be recognised that fate, in the sense of the appearance of undesired events, represents an enormous challenge for people, just as every illness, as a key example of fate, will always remain a challenge. For in the first instance, illness calls everything into question, it demands, challenges and compels us towards a fresh orientation. Therapeutic understanding alone no longer helps here; what is required is an appreciation of heart-felt recognition, a *raison du cœur,* by which one can delicately sense where a mutual path might lie, in order to penetrate into the deeper layers of the person in distress. As long as one allows for it, this path can lead to a genuine encounter, which helps sick people to find their way back to a good life, even in a situation where there is no cure: to another form of health, where being ill is gradually no longer seen as the enemy that has to be cleared out of the way, but rather as something which is to be affirmed, dealt with, possibly even inwardly overcome. This can only succeed by taking the path of »acceptance of oneself« (Romano Guardini), alongside the tragedy which every illness brings.

In order to help people in crisis situations it is important to clarify for ourselves the fluctuating dividing-line between constructive action and the acceptance of a predetermination. Modern medical practice must find a balance between these two opposing poles. It will continue to perfect the means for fighting illnesses, but it must also develop a sense of proportion when the external battle becomes an obsession and when it must be complemented by a process of coping. Sick people need an approach to healing that frees up their ability to overcome their fate, which is there and cannot be changed, and must be recognised as a part of their life. Making people aware of an opportunity for coping is one of the core tasks of a humane medicine that is based on the importance of human relationships.

6. Trust: Or why we cannot enforce what is true

> »The most important things we entrust to others are the things that need more to prosper than simply not getting involved.«
>
> *Annette Baier*

In an age in which medical practice is increasingly being viewed as a business concern, attitudes to it are also changing. The correct delivery of verifiable goods is expected from a business. It is concerned with directives, enforceable rights, legal positions, and contractual relations. The relationship between doctor and patient undoubtedly also has a contractual content, which cannot be overlooked. Medical treatment must comply with standards and rules, which for the most part are prescribed and indirectly even legally binding. However, medical action cannot be based entirely on a contractual relationship because it relies on both following rules as well as, in its dealings with individual patients, making singular and creative decisions, which do not follow any standardised schemata. Seriously ill patients ultimately hope to be treated by professionals who not only fulfil their contractual duties, but whom they can also trust as a person. It is human empathy which makes the contact between someone in need of help and a trained helper a viable relationship of trust. In medical practice, where highly rationalised procedures are gradually replacing interpersonal relationships, it is becoming increasingly difficult to find trust. In this chapter, we will take a closer look at why trust remains vital.

Trust, essentially, is to be found in the tension between unconditionally entrusting oneself to someone and the danger of trauma. Precisely because of its fundamental capacity to traumatise us, we would prefer not to depend on trust at all. We sense that it makes us vulnerable and, from the moment that we are conscious of the act of trust, we feel this vulnerability. We live in an age in which we are no longer able to cope well with our own vulnerability and we give priority to the guarantee of security over the risk of trust. Hence the contractual safeguards, the accounting and the calculating approach to the world. Yet, the more we insist on safety guarantees, the more we have to teach ourselves indifference, for only this allows us to live in a mode where we are not dependent on trust. I believe that the more we take a calculating approach to the world and the less vulnerable we want to be, the more we run into the danger of failing to live up to life. That is to say: what is legally due to us is generally inadequate for the purposes of living a good life. A discrepancy arises between what is legally stipulated and what is humanly necessary. What is legally prescribed can only be a kind of basic stipulation, which in itself cannot give assurance to people. For the purposes of this necessary feeling of assurance, of trust in the future, of trust in the solidarity of others, even the social system, this legally recognised stipulation has to be reinforced by what we cannot demand: affection, empathy, and the personal assumption of responsibility. We cannot sign contracts for the purposes of guaranteeing ourselves affection or empathy. We cannot legally document trust and yet we need trust in order to live at all.

In order to pursue these ideas in more depth, we must first look at the concept of trust, in a systematic way by looking in particular at trust between people. Let us concentrate entirely on people and in this context there are various meanings of trust. I will attempt to summarise them in seven points.

1. Trust as an assumption of good motives

Interpersonal trust always relates to the character of a person and not to a specific action (which would refer to reliability); thus, when we say that we trust people, we instinctively assume that they have good motives. We not only assume a particular expertise and qualification, but also believe them to have a fundamentally trustworthy personality. Trust relates to attitudes not actions and therefore, it is important to differentiate between reliability and trustworthiness. Experiencing that a person is unreliable does not automatically mean they are not trustworthy and vice versa, someone who we identify as reliable does not necessarily have our trust. Trustworthiness simply demands more than reliability in actions; a conscientious and competent engineer is not necessarily a trustworthy babysitter. The term personality already implies that trust refers to an unchanging attitude. It implies that the characteristics that trust is based on are not random characteristics, but ones which can be developed beyond momentary circumstances. In this way, trustworthiness could be designated a virtue, since virtue constitutes a disposition that exists over time and adapts not only situationally but also contingently, hence does not disappear again with the next circumstantial situation.

Trust does not relate to one particular accomplishment, but rather to the whole person. In a sense, it presupposes that the person whom I trust shares my values, at least to some degree. It could be said that trust presupposes a mutual set of values. It does not require any particular skill, but rather a morally likeminded person. A core aspect of a relationship of trust consists in committing to the realisation of shared values.[1] It could be described as an interpersonal connection, which aims at the realisation of a shared good. When we trust, we express how we view the other person at the same time. We assume not only a good character, but also a particular attitude of goodwill from which a bond can develop. A bond which is founded on the sharing of common values, both emotional and moral. This is a crucial point, for when we trust, we trust based on the consistency of these moral convictions. This means we assume that these fundamental convictions of others will remain intact, come what may. It is exactly this which differentiates the interpersonal relationship of trust from the economic relationship of a mutual pursuit of interest.[2] When I trust I do not assume that the person I trust is following his or her own interests (which happen to coincide with mine). Instead I assume that the person maintains certain basic convictions, which will not simply be abandoned when certain circumstances arise that do not coincide with his or her interests. I do not assume opportunist behaviour. The implicit reason for my trust, the character, is not altered by time.

2. Trust as a blessing and a demand

Trusting someone is a great blessing, for essentially it is a strong expression of personal recognition. People who con-

---

[1] Cp. Martin Hartmann, *Die Praxis des Vertrauens.* (Frankfurt am Main: Suhrkamp 2011), p. 177 and p. 231.

[2] Giovanni Maio, *Gesundheit als Geschäftsmodell. Wie der Markt die Heilkunst abschafft.* (Frankfurt am Main: Suhrkamp, 2014).

fide in let me know that they consider me a good person, in whose hands they can place their own well-being without having to demand any guarantees. Hence, what goes hand in hand with trust is the requirement that we prove ourselves worthy of trust. This is an important point, for we are talking here, to a certain extent, about a »self-fulfilling expectation«[3] The more I trust people, the more I encourage their trustworthiness, because by trusting them I appeal to their morality. However, this appeal demands a very particular disposition and a very particular interpersonal relationship.

The idea that we »bestow« trust also makes it clear that trust is fundamentally inaccessible and thus cannot be demanded or forced. There is no entitlement to trust. We can count ourselves fortunate when someone trusts us; staking a claim to it would be to misjudge the special character of trust as a personal distinction. Feeling trusted is a personal distinction which one can only receive gratefully.

In this sense, trust boosts the other person and awakens an attitude which could be described as a fundamental readiness to be considerate.[4] Trust means expecting something good from others, and this expectation releases the fundamental willingness to act considerately. Trust effects nothing less than a moral obligation in the other person. In other words: trust ennobles. The ennobling effect of trust should not be underestimated as it contributes to a humanisation of society in its own way. This humanisation stems from the dimension of recognition which lies in bestowing trust. Trust

---

[3] Claus Offe, »Wie können wir unseren Mitbürgern vertrauen?« In: M. Hartmann and C. Offe (Eds.), *Vertrauen. Die Grundlage des sozialen Zusammenhalts.* (Frankfurt am Main: Campus 2001), pp. 241–294, here p. 254.

[4] Cp. Martin Hartmann, *Die Praxis des Vertrauens.* (Frankfurt am Main: Suhrkamp 2011), p. 179.

is an expression of recognition and thus a motivation to prove oneself worthy of recognition.

3. An approach beyond the calculable

Trust is an emotional attitude and has nothing to do with calculation. It is neither the result of a calculation nor of a deliberate decision,[5] but rather of a fundamental sentiment which arises in someone. Prior experiences can indeed play a role, but they are not »gathered« in order to decide at some point *when* to trust. It could even be said that the less I consider it necessary to reflect on it, the more trust there is – and vice versa, the more I have to reflect on trust, the more fragile and questionable it is. Trust does not mean assessing other people, but rather unreservedly engaging with them. Trust is unplanned. It does not simply arise out of nothing and it is by no means completely unfounded. Yet is not the result of a calculation. Rather, we could say it is the result of a practical power of judgment, of a particular world view, an atmosphere or a climate in which everything is incorporated. It could also be described as a mode in which we discover the world as a felt disposition or an internal mental state with which we approach others. We encounter the other person with an inner conviction with regard to his or her existence and action. Martin Hartmann points out that we do not trust on the basis of proof, but rather from an inner conviction, which requires no proof, but cannot bear any evidence to the contrary.[6] Trust

---

[5] Cp. Martin Hartmann, Wer hat unser Vertrauen verdient? Philosophische Kriterien der Vertrauenswürdigkeit. In: M. Fischer and I. Kaplow (Eds.), *Vertrauen im Ungewissen*. (Berlin/ Münster: LIT Verlag 2008), pp. 48–69.

[6] Cp. Ibid. and Diego Gambetta, »Kann man dem Vertrauen vertrauen?« In:

is a kind of advance service which is fragile and can be taken away at any time. We react extremely sensitively to signs of a lack of trustworthiness, but we nevertheless offer our trust spontaneously.

In short, trust is not a calculated investment;[7] like love and affection, it springs from an inner conviction.

However, what sets trust apart from love and affection is the fact that trust is communicated differently to affection. Affection is announced, it is expressed in words and has a wide variety of labels attached to it, whereas trust always remains implicit. We do not specifically make it a theme for by doing so we would, in a sense, be querying its existence. Trust resonates in our attitude towards others, it colours our relationship with the world, without us being explicitly aware of it. Consequently, trust always means the supposition of a continuity of the world and the supposition of a stability of contexts. Olli Lagerspetz described trust as a state in which we »somehow find ourselves«[8], just as we breathe in air, which is simply there, and which we only notice when there is a shortage. Trust resonates between people and only becomes an issue when doubt creeps in. Lagerspetz sums this up laconically: »Unquestioned certainty is silent.«[9]

Hence, trust has less to do with pragmatic objectivity than with interpersonal relationships and thus follows different laws to those of calculation. It is the individual relation-

---

M. Hartmann and C. Offe (Eds.), *Vertrauen. Die Grundlage des sozialen Zusammenhalts.* (Frankfurt am Main: Campus 2001), pp. 204–237.

[7] Claus Offe, Wie können wir unseren Mitbürgern vertrauen? In: M. Hartmann and C. Offe (Eds.), *Vertrauen. Die Grundlage des sozialen Zusammenhalts.* (Frankfurt am Main: Campus 2001), pp. 241–294, see also p. 253.

[8] Olli Lagerspetz, »Vertrauen als geistiges Phänomen«. In: Martin Hartmann and Claus Offe (Eds.), *Vertrauen. Die Grundlage des sozialen Zusammenhalts.* (Frankfurt am Main: Campus 2001), pp. 85–113, here p. 93.

[9] Ibid, see also, p. 93.

ship to another person which determines whether trust can flourish or not. For this reason, it cannot be ensured by making suitable provisions. Trust is not an object of management; it is fundamentally contingent upon it. It cannot be produced and guaranteed, but only received.

4. The Risk of Trust

In trust there always remains an element of uncertainty; otherwise it would not be trust, but rather an agreement. Hence, there is an inherent willingness to accept a gap in knowledge. The question of trust does not arise where everything is certain. People who trust accept that they cannot guarantee that the other person will take a particular course of action and yet they open themselves up to the relationship and trust that the other person will behave accordingly. For this reason, Niklas Luhmann has described trust as a »risky commitment«[10]. We forgo obtaining reassuring information and unconditionally take the risk of trusting. In this we can recognise a creative approach to the boundaries of predictability. Trust represents a constructive response to the inevitability of ignorance and non-transparency, a response that says that life holds no ultimate guarantees. When we trust, we can go beyond what is certain and evident and do more than what pure calculation would suggest. The control imperative is replaced by inner calmness, such that in the end trust has to be seen as a precondition for a good life.

A popular German phrase is: trust is good, but control is better. This superficial saying ignores the fact that the future is fundamentally distinguished by being uncontrollable, non-

---

[10] Niklas Luhmann, *Vertrauen.* (Konstanz/Munich: UVK 2014), p. 23.

transparent and open. People who would like to replace trust with control have to lock themselves away, so as not to encounter anything or anybody, since every encounter inevitably entails risks. Luhmann says that »without any kind of trust« a person could »not get out of bed in the morning ... anything would be possible.«[11] This clearly shows that, in a certain way, trust is a leap of defiance against life's inherent uncertainties. Without this leap it would be difficult to cope with the fundamentally open nature of our future. Trust entails the emotional bridging of a necessary lack of knowledge about the future, and the inner disposition not to view this as something crippling, but as something normal. To trust someone means to be tolerant with our fragmentary knowledge. Trust transforms the objective insufficiency of knowledge into a subjective certainty that life will »turn out well« even without guarantees.

Trust only comes into play when issues are important to us. For we can only, in the narrower sense, »entrust« something to another person that we feel strongly about. Since every person feels strongly about something, everyone must have an interest in being able to trust someone. In admitting to ourselves how much something means to us, we also discover that we are vulnerable, since in the moment of trusting someone we make ourselves dependent on their decisions, which we cannot control. We give others power over us or over what is dear to us, and at that moment discover our own defencelessness. Ignoring this dependence would be patently naïve. However, the distinctive feature of trust is that we freely choose this dependence. Along with becoming conscious of our dependence there is an acceptance of our vulnerability. People, who want to be invulnerable, are condemned to never being able to trust, they will lapse into a spiral of

---

11 Ibid., p. 1.

control and ultimately become incapable of action. Therefore, trust is a constructive way of dealing with one's own vulnerability. At the same time, it points to a person's inescapable dependency, because it is not possible to live without believing in the good character of other people and being able to emotionally rely upon them.

5. Trust in contrast to a contractual relationship

When we place our trust in someone, we ignore meticulous instructions, we leave it to them to gauge what needs to be done. Placing your trust in someone means recognising that action cannot be entirely pre-structured. Rather than formalising, we place our trust in the ability of the people we trust to evaluate the situation themselves.[12] We trust them to take care of that which we have entrusted them competently and responsibly. The special feature of trust is its implicitness: its implementation is unconditionally placed in the hands of the others, which means at the same time that they are granted their own space and freedom to act.

Hence, trust is the opposite of a specific agreement that determines in an explicit and detailed fashion what is to be done. Precisely this point clearly expresses the difference between a relationship based on trust and a contractual relationship. As we have seen, in trusting we accept vulnerability, whilst a contract aims at minimising vulnerability. The basis of a contract is always an abstract contractual item, such as supplying goods or a service, which is not unconditionally entrusted to someone, but rather, in case of doubt, can be

[12] Cp. Martin Hartmann, *Die Praxis des Vertrauens*. (Frankfurt am Main: Suhrkamp 2011), p. 219.

settled legally. Contractual partners are addressed formally: the people who have to fulfil the terms of a contract can be named, but they neither figure in person nor in their relation to each other. Individual discretion is replaced by clearly defined guidelines, which must be interpreted in terms of the contract. What is implicit, situationally dependent and personal in a relationship of trust, takes on an explicit, schematic and legally enforceable character in a contract. In short, every contract is formalistic and as such provides security, but at the cost of the loss of an interpersonal relationship.

The relationship between the respective contractual partners is precisely detailed in the contract; it does not allow for interpretations and deviations and it is concluded on payment and delivery. Human relationships, feelings of commitment or guilt have no place here, for the exchange, which is laid down in the objective form of a contract, is directly characterised by the strict independence of the exchanging partners. In other words, following the successful conclusion of such an exchange, we find ourselves, as it were, in an empty space. We entered into the relationship with our contractual partner in a notional way, and in the same notional way we leave it. We expect no personal or even moral feelings of commitment from our contractual partner, and conversely none of gratitude. Both are unnecessary, as the contractual requirements have all already been met. The French philosopher Marcel Hénaff describes a contract as an »exchange of mundane life«[13]. Contractual relationships may suffice with regard to objects, in medical practice, however, we are dealing with people. Since people who are ill, in particular, need more than just a pragmatic service, a contract can provide a framework

---

[13] Marcel Hénaff, *Der Preis der Wahrheit. Gabe, Geld und Philosophie.* (Frankfurt am Main: Suhrkamp 2009), p. 474.

but cannot provide the feeling of being in good hands or the feeling of dignity.

6. The undermining of trust through economisation

Contracts are drawn up to project self-interest. The implementation of each party's self-interest is, in fact, the essential feature of a contract. This makes it the opposite of a social commitment which is, to a large extent, made redundant by the precise definition of the contractual terms. A contract includes neither empathy nor a willingness to help and also takes no account of the well-being of the other contractual partner. Fulfilling one's contractual duties is all that is required and, of course, in one's own interest. Adam Smith, the founder of modern economics, encapsulated this clearly and unambiguously: »It is not from the benevolence of the butcher, the brewer or the baker, that we expect our dinner, but from their regard to their own interest. We address ourselves not to their humanity but to their self-love.«[14]

The pervading intrusion of purely economic thinking in medical practice is increasingly leading to the loss not only of trust but also of personal trustworthiness. Trustworthiness is lost when doctors are called upon to ask themselves, when treating a patient, whether the patient will amount to something for them. The patient is used as the key factor in making ends meet. The fact that this means a reversal in the ac-

[14] Adam Smith, *An inquiry into the Nature and Causes of the Wealth of Nations*, Ed. R. H. Campbell and A. S. Skinner. 2 vols. Glasgow Edition of the Works and Correspondence of Adam Smith 2. (Oxford University Press, 1976), p. 19.

tual point of medical treatment is scarcely considered, or at best vaguely felt. Trust is replaced by calculation. When we bear in mind that a business concern is intrinsically based on the calculation of its own interests and turnover is judged on this calculation, it becomes clear that transforming medical practice into an industrial concern means losing all the values which have nothing to do with this »austere« calculating orientation towards one's own interests.

This demonstrates how much modern medical practice has become alienated from its quintessential task, without consciously realising it. To some extent, we only realise this when doctors lapse into an existential crisis concerning the gradual undermining of relationships of trust within medical practice. This erosion of trust between doctor and patient along with the loss of trust of health insurers in a doctor's specific expertise can only be measured inadequately using standardised guidelines and which demands more than can be organised at a contractual level. Doctors need, above all, to feel that they are doing something worthwhile, that they are performing a meaningful task; and the point of the task results from being aware that they are there for others and can be deemed to be trustworthy in their action. They rely on the fact that they work in a system where they are able to do the right thing, not for the purposes of external gratification, but for the purposes of the good feeling of being able to enter into a relationship with their patients. A relationship that allows them to demonstrate, in equal measure, their professional competence, their experience and their human empathy in their care for others. Such a relationship requires mutual trust. However, it also requires that the doctor invests more than just the minimum legal requirement. This process of complete contractualisation is, therefore, an expression of the undermining of the tasks of a doctor. Taken to its logical conclusion, it is the result of a devaluation of the medical profession, which is then not associated with interpersonal relationships, but rather formal service provision.

There is no denying that medical practice cannot be carried out without guaranteed standards and hence contractual relationships. Every patient has the right to appropriate care, to specific standards and the security of a legally guaranteed medical system. However, a contractual relationship is doomed to be superficial: a contract is binding, yet does not bind people together. If we rely entirely on the contract, i.e. on pertinence and relevant rights, we introduce nothing other than the idea of an »essential indifference« in human relationships, since with the idea of a mere exchange of goods we validate a type of right to indifference. The more a contract is lauded as a central paradigm, the more this social question is reduced to an »effective sociality« (Marcel Hénaff), where personal ties are no longer of primary importance, but instead the observance of rules. For service provision automatically creates distance; ultimately out of the interpersonal relationship between a patient and a doctor it is to facilitate a »personal service« between two parties. In doing this, we overlook the fact that the doctor-patient relationship, particularly when it involves serious illnesses, cannot reasonably be viewed as anything other than a profound form of human companionship. It could possibly even be said that for a seriously ill person, this interpersonal relationship represents something so precious that it is beyond an estimable value.

In the comparison between trust and contract it has become clear that what is gained through trust cannot be replaced by any contract. Without trust there is no feeling of affinity or of being in safe hands, no experienced solidarity and no feeling of moral unity. This brings us to the final point.

7. The power of trust to foster community

As Georg Simmel maintains, trust is without doubt »one of the most important synthetic forces within society«.[15] Co-operation and community are only possible through trust, for each of us would be incapable of taking in the almost limitless amount of information needed to completely guarantee a co-operation or relationship with someone. If we did not relentlessly invest in the emotional advance offering of trust, we would be incapable of action and maintaining a relationship. Only trust enables relationships and gives them depth. It has a cohesive power, and at the same time, the potential to humanise a society, because it releases good feelings and increases the willingness to become actively involved in a shared good.

Trust could be described as a fundamental quality very close to a virtue. What differentiates it from other virtues is that it requires a balance between healthy mistrust and a fundamental disposition to trust. People who preclude the possibility of being able to trust and become fixed on mere control, will neither be able to enter into relationships nor co-operate with anyone. They will in this way be excluded from a greater scope of happiness and success. Pure mistrust leads to a loss of possibilities and to »wasted opportunities« (Russel Hardin)[16] We are connected to other people by our ability to trust and so we expand the scope of our own possible course of action. Because trust is ultimately nothing more than the

---

[15] Georg Simmel, *Soziologie. Untersuchungen über die Formen der Vergesellschaftung.* Gesamtausgabe, Vol.11, ed. by Otthein Rammstedt. (Frankfurt am Main: Suhrkamp 1992 [1908]), p. 263.

[16] Russell Hardin, »Die Alltagsepistemologie von Vertrauen«. In: Martin Hartmann and Claus Offe (Eds.), *Vertrauen. Die Grundlage des sozialen Zusammenhalts.* (Frankfurt am Main: Campus 2001), pp. 295–332, here p. 298.

willingness to enter into relationships that are beyond our control, a life of constant mistrust would create an attitude where relationships would be prevented from arising.

Particularly when we consider this context, it seems impossible to lead a full life, even just a life with other people, without trust, and so we have no other choice but to trust. We must possess a healthy sense of trust, not go about it blindly. We can and must protect ourselves from the disappointment of a breach of trust by means of experience, judgment and intuition, but, at the same time, we should reject the idea that trust can only be given if we safeguard ourselves in all matters of human concern. Trust is a kind of intermediary state between ignorance and knowledge. People who trust know something, even if they often cannot find a name for this. Referring to Georg Simmel we could summarise as follows: Someone who knows everything, *does not need* to trust; on the other hand, someone who knows absolutely nothing *cannot* trust.

Of course, we desire security, but enforced security can only ever exist when it is formalised. Yet the most important things in life do not require formalistic assistance, but rather trustworthy people who concern themselves with them. It is, therefore, the task of medical practice not only to satisfy contractual and professional requirements, but also to realise that it must strive to gain trust. A patient relies on trustworthy medical practice; trustworthiness that can be seen in a doctor's good and caring motives which lie beyond self-interest and at the same time the ability to carry out concrete measures to help based on these benevolent motives. Good motives, which enable the doctor to respond adequately to the patient's needs through this fundamental attitude and disposition. For it is benevolence that marks a doctor's action as an integral part of a human community and from which a patient can gain strength and draw hope. At least hope that this benevolence, regardless of what happens and or what comes of it, will remain unchanged.

Consequently, absolute trust is directly connected with the topic of hope. We can only experience trust if we have hope. This demonstrates how important it is to address the topic of hope, particularly in the case of severe chronic illnesses. The next chapter will examine this very point do.

7. The Therapeutic Goal of Hope: What hope can mean for modern medicine

»Despair is more treacherous than hope.«
Luc de Clapiers, Marquis de Vauvenargues

When I was a young doctor, I once had to inform and talk to a patient about her incurable illness. After we had discussed everything she said: »Then we'll just have to hope.« This answer fascinated me and I wondered for a long time what she could have meant by it. Over time I realised that this patient had fully understood what hope was all about. In this case, her answer made me aware that hope is a subject which has to do with the treatment of patients. Modern medical practice concentrates on pragmatic approaches, but focuses far too little on existential questions, even though it is these questions which concern people when they are seriously ill.

In the first instance, it seems difficult to talk about something like hope. We live in an age where the courage to hope has been lost because our life is permeated by the idea of planning and guarantees. In our society shaped by science, technology and economics, there is a bias towards what is calculable. Day after day it is instilled into us that only strategic action is the right action. In this scenario, hope is in a difficult position, since the future, which it is oriented towards, is now a present prolonged by calculation and not a genuinely open future. Science and technology make the future appear predictable as a result of demonstrable natural laws. Anyone who talks about hope within this understanding of the world arouses suspicion and will be said to be short-sighted: short-sighted by not obtaining sufficient information and making provisions for the future. Today, management has replaced hope and consequently hope has become *passé*. Now that functionality and causality are considered the relevant criteria for making decisions, there are only imperatives, probabilities and forecasts, but no there is no real hope. Modern medical practice also focuses on numbers, on control and on calculation; it can produce prognoses but not hope in the sense of trusting the future. Scientific thought has to be limited to what is determinable in order to be able to make scientific propositions at all. However, the disproportionate concentration on what can be determined inevitably leads to a narrowing of the horizon of reality. In short, we live in an age in which we would rather crunch numbers than foster hope. Certainly, none of us will want to give up calculation and replace it only with hope; but just calculating without hoping is simply not enough to be able to live.

In order to clarify the existential meaning of hope in a medical context, we should, first of all, approach the concept in an entirely systematic way. What is hope? We differentiate between tangible hope directed towards a particular good, and a generally held »hopeful disposition«. Otto Friedrich Bollnow also described the latter as universal hope. Luise Rinser, in her book *Über die Hoffnung* (1964) (English: *About Hope*), differentiates between »hoping that« and »being hopeful«, and the philosopher Alois Edmaier also writes about »objective hope«, as opposed to »fundamental hope«. Whilst objective hope means the expectation of a particular good in the future in the sense of »everyday hope«, »fundamental hope« represents the existential layer of consciousness, which definite hope makes possible in the first place. In this regard, the French language differentiates semantically between *espoir*, as being changeable hope, and *espérance* as being fundamental hope. This first important differentiation should not, however, detract from the connection between both forms of hope. According to this connection, we can only hope in a concrete fashion when we are driven by a principal hope. People »choose« their everyday hopes on the basis of a hope which drives and directs them. But what exactly is this hope? I would firstly like to continue this systematic analysis in order to then elucidate the meaning of hope for modern medical practice.

Hope as a realistic relation to the future

As the philosopher Helmut Fahrenbach puts it; »Hope always involves reaching into the future«.[1] We hope for something that is still pending. We can also hope that something in the past might not have happened, but even then we are not hoping for the past, but for the future. People live with the mind directed to an open future. They are being oriented towards the future; the visualisation of what lies ahead tomorrow determines their today. Since the future is never certain and thus remains largely inaccessible, people are reliant on being able to hope for the future they need in order to shape their present. We all live in hope.

Yet we can only hope for something which is principally attainable. Something which is unattainable *per se,* cannot be an object of hope. For instance, we can certainly hope to get better (at something) but we cannot hope to remain young forever. That would be more like a utopian vision, a wish or a longing, but not hope. Hope has nothing to do with wishful

---

[1] Helmut Fahrenbach, *Wesen und Sinn der Hoffnung. Versuch über ein Grenzphänomen zwischen philosophischer und theologischer Daseinsauslegung.* (Typoskript: Heidelberg 1955), p. 59.

thinking. For we are all completely free in our wishes, but when we speak of hope, we are referring to something which is fundamentally feasible. Here we come to a crucial point which is an obstacle to modern-day discussion on hope. Hope is often associated with illusionary thinking, whilst, in fact, the opposite is the case. A particular characteristic of hope is that it is able to surmount the purely calculatorial approach to the world and understands reason to be more than a purely instrumental form of calculation. Hope does indeed assume a calculation, but it does not stop there. Thus, hope is less of a strategic action than an attitude, and in fact an attitude towards the unpredictability of the future.

On the other hand, the unpredictability of the future makes it difficult to hope. For instance, there is illusory, unexplained and even blind hope, but is blind hope really still hope? It is important to distinguish in conceptual terms between hope, wishful thinking, daydreaming and a utopian vision. Unlike the latter, hope has clear sight of what »actually is«. It does not ignore reality but instead recognises it, and because it clearly recognises the inadequacies of the present, it is fundamentally reason-oriented. Therefore, a characteristic of hope is that it does not gloss over adverse reality but rather affirms it, but in such a way that it does not allow itself to be overwhelmed by it. In other words, people who hope, see more than what is offered. They recognise possibilities in the inherently adverse, and so hope is not insufficient knowledge, but rather the ability to see more. Gerhard Sauter described it as a kind of intuition for the positive possibilities the future has in store.[2] A person hoping is a person seeing clearly. Someone who creates perspectives. Nineteenth-century dictionaries even describe hope as semantically asso-

[2] Gerhard Sauter, *Erwartung und Erfahrung*. (Munich: Kaiser 1972), p. 73.

ciated with the light of hope.[3] It is precisely this double meaning, on the one hand a keen eye for reality and on the other hand a sense of possibility, which makes hope so fascinating.

Hope as an acknowledgment of the limits of our power to control

I would describe hope as the link between rationality and humility. Humility, in the sense that people who hope are fully aware that the future is inaccessible and their access to it cannot be completely planned and guaranteed. We are not responsible for the future, it happens *to* us. So we can only talk about hope when we find ourselves in a situation which is characterised by uncertainty and uncontrollability. What differentiates hope from expectation is the degree of certainty with which we can foresee a future event. If we were relatively certain that something would occur, we would talk about expectation, not hope. Hence, we can hope for a cure, but by contrast we would expect the scheduled arrival of a bus and not hope for it. Hope only comes into play when something is difficult to attain or its appearance is rather more unlikely.

It is not only the uncertainty that what we hoped for will come true that characterises hope. It is also always a matter of recognising that hoping is dependent on circumstances that cannot be influenced, on a stroke of luck or the help of a third party. When we hope, we recognise that the end result does not simply depend on our action. In short, hoping implies the

[3] Ralf Lutz, *Der hoffende Mensch. Anthropologie und Ethik menschlicher Sinnsuche.* (Bern: Francke 2012), p. 159.

recognition of the limits of our power to control. It is related to moments which are beyond our own sphere of control. The French philosopher Gabriel Marcel expresses it as follows: »The only real sense of hope is one that is directed at something which is not in our hands.«[4] Hope is linked with recognising the boundaries of what is feasible, predictable and calculable. These ideas can be encapsulated as follows: only having a boundary allows people to hope.

When we hope, we move in a kind of limbo: we know very well that the future cannot be completely influenced by our action, but we are convinced that it appears realisable. It is all about the inner attitude towards unavoidably fragmentary knowledge. In a way hope gives us the strength to endure the irrevocable limbo of human existence and thus remain capable of acting in situations of uncertainty.

Hope as not being fixated on something

Josef Pieper describes hope as »being open to something of which you neither know the hour nor the form of its fulfilment.«[5] This could also be expressed in a more positive light: hope does not shut itself off from what is coming because by definition it does not already determine what *should* come. Hope comprises the idea of a future that is open. It has something to do with being able to infer. It is to do with the ability to be open to things. This affirmative attitude makes it possible to even envision the future *in* the present, and that

---

[4] Gabriel Marcel, *Philosophie der Hoffnung*. (Munich: List 1957), p. 45.

[5] Josef Pieper, »Über die Hoffnung der Kranken«. In: M.-P. Engelmeier (Ed.), *Von der Hoffnung der Kranken*. (St. Augustin: Verlag Wort und Werk 1977), pp. 13–34, here p. 33.

way to »have« future. People who hope do not look towards a particular future nor do they tie it down to a projectable conclusion, but rather let the future happen and remain open for what might come. In other words, they make the future possible simply by allowing it to happen. They impose no conditions on it. They do not insist on a narrowly defined content upon which the sense of their life then depends; they trust. They trust that even when what they long for so fiercly does not come to pass, there will still be something which allows them to live. Consequently, people who hope trust less in a favourable chain of events and more in the fact that they will be able to react inwardly, regardless of what happens. They trust in their inner strength not to break under something unforeseeable.

Hoping means being open to the future, confident of being able to cope with what is in store. Hope is geared less towards future content than to the actual self. In a more profound sense we do not hope for »something« but rather for our own self. We hope to be strong enough for the future. This is the difference between hoping and planning. When we plan we extrapolate our current expectations and place them in the future. By contrast, when we hope we let the future happen and are ready to accept it as *our* future.

It is precisely this aspect which is of particular significance for medical practice. We have seen that hope is in a difficult position. This has primarily to do with the fact that we have lost our connection to an open future today. We can scarcely bear not knowing exactly what tomorrow will bring. We immerse ourselves in planning down to the last detail, in calculating probabilities and making prognoses, in order to get to grips with an open future. This will never succeed, as the future is characterised by being inaccessible, always and at any time. We can only really live well when we learn to accept this inaccessibility and adapt to it. This ability to adapt to a fundamentally open space is called hope. So perhaps this is a better way to understand why, today, we live in a »hopeless« time and why medical practice focuses so much on prognosis and so little on hope. It too cannot tolerate this openness and so takes refuge in scientism.

There is another important aspect to this: by means of its technical approach, medical practice determines in advance what the aim of the treatment should be. It thereby restricts both its own and the patient's view of a future to one based solely on the point of view of probability. Probabilities, however, can only be calculated with regard to what has already been determined as the future we can expect. If we were to think freely about it, we would have to recognise that, fundamentally, we cannot know what to hope, as we cannot completely pre-structure the future. The more we adopt a scientific and technical approach to having become ill, the more we limit the radius of our imagination and become fixated on the areas we can outline probabilistically and technically. The technically induced attitude of expectation restricts future horizons to a considerable degree and obscures everything which cannot be calculated and planned, but which, nevertheless, can happen.

However, this scientific and technical approach misleads the patient not only into adopting this limited perspective, but also into fixating on it and becoming increasingly unable to deviate from the seemingly predictable future and seek out uncharted areas. Much like the doctor who professes to be a technician and provider of procedures, the patient is also persuaded to adopt expectation and forgets how to hope. Exclusively reverting to expectation entails shutting oneself off. It narrows horizons and incentivises demands for control. The more medical practice masquerades as purely technical and purposively rational, the more it results in a limited view and a patient's self-isolation.

The patient's statement quoted earlier: »Then we'll just have to hope«, expressed the view that she remained open to what might come, but at the same time hoped that what was to come would be in some way good. She trusted in something which she could not quantify at all, simply from an inner certainty. This was possible because the relationship of trust that had been established in our conversation (which was not geared towards a concrete expectation) allowed for such feelings of confidence and security. So, in crisis situations, we are well-advised not to limit hope to a particular goal, but rather to see it as what it essentially is: an openness for what may happen and trust in the fact that it can be mastered.

Hope as Patience

When people hope, they create a particular relationship to time. Someone who hopes adopts an attitude to time, to which a person not hoping does not have access: the willingness to be patient, the ability just to let things happen and to »trust in the process of growing and maturing«.[6] Thus, hope prevents sullenness and despair. When we hope we know of the incalculability of the future; we do not, of course, know what will happen, but we have an internal willingness to overcome this state of not-knowing through patience. Hope is different from rebellion and also despair in that it enables patience and prevents someone from forcing the issue or prematurely writing something off. Perhaps hope could be described as having respect for time, as an acknowledgement

[6] Gabriel Marcel, *Philosophie der Hoffnung*. (Munich: List 1957), see also, p. 43.

that a process of transition is inherent in time, that things change and that from the moment we lose hope we forfeit this respect for time and incline towards impatience. Gabriel Marcel powerfully illustrates that despair is fundamentally nothing more than an act of impatience: »It goes without saying that that is the same despair which forces me to declare that I can never be healthy […]. However, it does seem to be that when I hope, as regards what occurs and above all what this occurrence makes of me, I develop a type of relationship, a kind of trustworthiness, comparable to the attitude I have towards another person when I am patient with him.«[7] This thought shows that hope is nothing other than the ability to summon up patience with a view to our own fate. Patience becomes possible by not only looking at the future in a different way, but above all by looking at the present in a different way. Whilst a desperate person limits the present to the »not-yet«, and so remains trapped in it, a person who hopes, recognises, despite the deficient present, the fundamental possibility of good. In this way, people who hopes »have« more future than those who do not because they understand the present as a possibility for the future and thus know how to envision it in the here and now. Patience is the art of envisioning the future whilst in the present.

This context also allows us to recognise the one-sidedness and inadequacies of the developments in modern medical practice. Due to economisation, medical practice has manoeuvred itself into a situation where time has become the first thing that is sacrificed to efficiency and profitability: time for waiting patiently and allowing for the situation to develop. The result is not waited for, but instead is forced through action. However, by rationalising away time, people's ability to hope is also rationalised away. It slips back, as

[7] Ibid.

it were, into Pandora's Box. Where an attitude of giving oneself time is not encouraged, there remains no room for hope, nor for consolation. This results in a vicious circle, as the tendency to speed things up and the emphasis on action make hope impossible, and yet at the same time they are results of not being able to hope. Where hope is absent, the emphasis on action steps in.

Hope as an impetus for action

In light of this, it could be tempting to contrast hope with spirited action, organising and doing things. A particular characteristic of hope, however, is that it is not the opposite of action, but rather a part of it. Hope is, therefore, not to be confused with merely waiting, it includes the impetus to organise. As the theologian Ralf Lutz once put it, »Hope is an active reach into the future.«[8] Consequently, it is not a case of composure, but instead a case of reaching out and preparing for the future, for a future that one can bring about »actively«.

Alois Edmaier encapsulates the value of hope when he writes: »If a wish is the father of thought, then hope is the mother of the deed.«[9] For people who hope, a good future has the character of an obligation. They are concerned with contributing to this possible future. They are certainly not resigned to fate, fatalistically, resigned to what will come, instead they trust in a good future and for precisely this reason

---

8 Ralf Lutz, *Der hoffende Mensch. Anthropologie und Ethik menschlicher Sinnsuche.* (Bern: Francke 2012), p. 431.

9 Alois Edmaier, *Horizonte der Hoffnung.* (Regensburg: Pustet 1968), p. 143.

are happy to espouse it. Paul Ricœur describes hope as the »passion for the possible«[10] and stresses that this passion is unavoidably rooted in »real aspirations«. The hopeful visualisation of something better in the future does not lead to passivity, but instead to shaping the present.

What becomes clear is that there is a relationship between hope and freedom. The philosopher Richard Schaeffler defines human freedom as »the power to make concrete, yet relative and provisional choices for action transparent for the aims hope wishes to attain«.[11] Only by the courage to act, which hope confers, will people be able to make use of their freedom. Hope protects us from resignation and hence protects us in anticipating failure, from not making use of our freedom for action. By deferring certain aims to the wide expanse of the future, hope confers freedom to people to think beyond the factual, to consider alternatives, to be open to the future, and thus to think and act with open eyes.

Hope as acknowledgement of one's own vulnerability

Another preconception levelled against hope needs to be questioned. Hoping sounds like glorifying, embellishing and romanticising. Yet on closer examination it is exactly the opposite. This becomes evident when we look at the time when hope becomes a topic for discussion. If life is comfortable, hope is not an issue. It only comes into play if our health is affected, if we are frightened and feel threatened. For this

[10] Paul Ricœur, *Hermeneutik und Psychoanalyse. Der Konflikt der Interpretationen II.* (Munich: Kösel-Verlag 1984), p. 113.

[11] Richard Schaeffler, »Zur Anthropologie und Ethik der Hoffnung«. In: *Münchner Theologische Zeitschrift*, vol. 33, no.1, (1982), pp. 1–24, here p. 8.

reason, hope is a central issue for people who are ill. Hence, talking about hope signifies also recognising that we feel threatened, in danger or full of fear. There is a good reason why, in conversation, we pair the words hope and fear. Gabriel Marcel sums it up as follows: »The basis of hope is knowledge of a situation which makes us despair.«[12] When we hope, we are confronted with a distressful situation, with the danger of losing the ground under our feet. Helmut Fahrenbach also describes hope as the »answer to a problematic situation«.[13] In this situation of radical uncertainty and irresolvable fear, people who hope extends into the underlying structure of being itself. From this descent into the depths of their being, they become aware of what gives them the power to trust in the fact that, even in times of futility and failure, not everything will be meaningless.

In order to understand this, it can be helpful to compare hope to another concept, which it is often confused with, optimism. Optimists are people who do not seriously consider despair an option. They view reality without regard for its potential tragedy and thus act fearlessly, swiftly and even naively. Hope is exactly the opposite of this, because it arises where facileness, light-heartedness and recklessness have been torn apart. In this state, the person hoping does not shy away from things, but wants to see everything. Rooted within hope is a kind of clear-sightedness, which evades the optimist who is full of certainty. A person who hopes sees the many horizons of possibility, as well as the danger of, indeed even the questionability of existence. Thesepeople who hope live in an area of tension between fear and confidence with-

[12] Gabriel Marcel, *Sein und Haben.* (Paderborn: Schöningh 1954), p. 80.
[13] Helmut Fahrenbach, *Wesen und Sinn der Hoffnung. Versuch über ein Grenzphänomen zwischen philosophischer und theologischer Daseinsauslegung.* (Typoskript. Heidelberg 1955), p. 68.

out being able to exchange one for the other. Their basic feeling is not one of conviction, but rather of ambivalence, and it is precisely this which enables a deeper understanding of their existence.

Hope as trust and understanding of what is meaningful

As soon as we hope, we show with this hope that there is a reason which supports us. However, this reason for hoping cannot be identified or explained. It is a part of the person who hopes; it cannot be produced or justified, only discovered. Hoping refers to a fundamental reason for being, to what motivates people to carry on. In other words, the real reason for hoping is not that certain something we hope for, it is in fact that we trust that we have a worthwhile future, whatever it might be. Thus, hope is nothing more than trust in future possibilities, that even in the utmost despair, the final word has not yet been spoken. A person who hopes expresses, in that hope, trust, namely trust in the fact that there is something worth living for.

Viewed in a more fundamental way, hope is a type of solution to the existential state of mind of a person, who being human can never possess complete certainty. This trust cannot refer to verifiable knowledge, but rather is an idea which comes from deep inside a person, or is implicit knowledge. Gabriel Marcel describes it as »supralogical knowledge«. It could also be called conviction, for there is a lot more to conviction than rational calculation. Marcel compares it to an advance or a credit which a person grants because this person longs for unity and cannot refrain from looking forward to the future, confident of being able to become whole. This advance affects the human condition as such: A person strives for fulfilment, and fulfilment means discovering wholeness and overcoming the fragmentary nature of being. When hoping, this primeval human need takes effect and is converted into assertive action.

By pointing out possibilities intuitively and trusting in a fundamental reason, hope has the potential to overcome existential fear. When we hope, it is possible to discover emotional security within the perception of the fundamental fragility of human existence and this is translated into meaningfulness.

Human hope is based on a reason that is related to the deep-rooted desire for wholeness within a person's being. This desire to overcome what is fragmentary and contradictory is a striving, which has nothing to do with personal preferences, but rather with human existence itself. Thus, hope is an anthropological constant and not a result of external circumstances. It is a part of the human being, because humans, each in their own way, strive after wholeness.

Hope, being »existential«, is invariably linked to the question of meaning. People who hope do not get caught up in particulars, but instead enquire after the meaning of the whole, and can only transcend harsh reality if they integrate this ultimate meaning into their »real striving«, as Ricœur termed it. Hope is the internalisation of a prospect of meaning, trusting in the fact that the wholeness of life does not remain meaningless even in the face of adversity.

This demonstrates that when we hope, we come to understand something about ourselves. Prompted by the question of our being, we begin to give ourselves a purpose. In this way, hope is less of a final answer and more of a state where we open ourselves up to this question of the meaning of life. Hope leads us towards understanding ourselves. Helmut Fahrenbach described it appropriately as »finding oneself«. Finding oneself within a horizon which encompasses the whole of existence.

All hope is community

So what could hope play in modern medical practice? Hope represents a lifesaving resource for reflecting on human existence. But where will we get that hope from? It cannot simply be brought to the patients from outside. It ultimately remains inaccessible. Yet hope is not something which is either there or not; hope is a *process*, a process of finding oneself. When we are critically ill, our initial hope is to be cured. This initial and totally natural impulse cannot be denied or contradicted. We seek support in the hope of recreating what was previously self-evident. Over time, however, we have to recognise that there is not only this kind of hope. Numerous studies have shown that people who have become aware of the fact that their illness is incurable begin to hope, but in a different way. This is the processual nature of hoping. The problem with modern medical practice is that it inhibits this process by not going past the first step.

When a cure can no longer be found, hope does not end; it is only just beginning. Only then does the situation of distress become so severe that we search for a fundamental reason for our existence. We need support in our search, not in the shape of offering hope, but by being shown that it is worth enquiring further in our search of a fundamental reason and to painstakingly seek that reason in our reality.

When someone becomes ill and medical cure is ineffectual, they can either draw upon hope or fall into despair. Both are a part of human nature. Hope is certainly not something which is simply there. What is simply there is, in fact, the feeling of menace and of being in danger and precisely this becomes particularly powerful during the illness. It is, therefore, a question of whether this feeling remains or if we, somewhere, find a reason to hope, not an objective and demonstrable reason, but one which is within us in our attitude towards the world. In all of life's situations, every single person can be confident that, despite a bad prognosis, they can still find comfort in the knowledge that they are supported by something, whether it be a loved one, or the knowledge that they are able to leave something behind, be it through encounters with other people, who in their own small way have changed something. Ultimately, hope is about trusting in the fact that something which is close to someone's heart will endure (see the section on trust). It is about trusting in the continuity of something meaningful. It is also about being allowed to hope for community, which itself is something supportive, because within it we can discover how precious it can be (still) to be alive.

Only individual answers can be found here. Answers which come from within. However, I am fully convinced that every person, even those who do not believe in life after death, can hope. They can hope that, from somewhere, they will gain the strength to overcome the challenge of their illness and its accompanying suffering. They can hope that they will not be alone and that, even in this situation there can be emotional security in knowing that they mean something to other people. Ultimately, it is about hoping for help, but not help in the one-sided sense of cure or repair, but in the sense of a helping community, a community which itself can be supportive, because one feels protected and a part of it and gains a feeling for the preciousness of a life still to live.

Therefore, if nothing else, hope can be understood to be a result of relationships with other people. We cannot hope by ourselves in isolation: we need the feeling that there is someone out there who believes in us. Without the experience of someone connecting with us, hope is barely possible. So hope always includes a dimension of community, and for exactly this reason people who are seriously ill rely existentially on a form of medical practice that does not exclude conversation and relationship. Martin Hildebrandt, the Munich-based doctor, writes: »The healing process does not lay claim to success, but to the attempt at success and this cannot only work in community with others, but will undoubtedly fail spectacularly in cases of loneliness. To promise more than an attempt would be unfair, however, someone who does not try has already lost. […] The offer of companionship is the minimum requirement that must be demanded from the healing process […] The moment when the healing process fails, in the face of death, is often a difficult challenge to bear. However, it is nothing in comparison to the fear of dying alone. To hope for healing is to hope for companionship.«[14]

It becomes increasingly clear that hope, ultimately, has a dialogical character by nature. It remains dependent on »an informal you« and on interpersonal relationships. Gabriel Marcel describes »we-encounters« as the basis of all hope.[15] And it is precisely these encounters which provide the potential for the relationship between a doctor and a patient. When a doctor-patient contact succeeds in becoming an encounter in the true sense of a »we-encounter«, there is room for hope.

We live in an age where talk of high hopes appears suspicious and where we prefer to speak of the small chances of success. We respond to life's crises with operational technology and pragmatic procedures and so we choose to attempt to

---

[14] Martin Hildebrandt. »Heilungsprozesse in der Kunst«, In: *TRIGON 11. Kunst, Wissenschaft und Glaube im Dialog*. Ed. by the Guardini Stiftung. (Berlin: BWV 2014), pp. 65–78, here p. 77.

[15] Gabriel Marcel, *Philosophie der Hoffnung*. (Munich: List 1957), p. 71.

control rather than ask where there could be a reason for greater hope. Modern hope is the hope to be able to control the future and to make it absolutely certain. Strictly speaking this is not actually hope, but rather an expression of hopelessness. The more we subject the future to prognostics, the more we behave like people in distress, i. e. people who have lost their basic confidence in an open future. This veiled form of the inability to hope is also demonstrated in how we deal with illness. We tend to place hope in the favourable influence of external determinants, and forget that we, as humans, have been given the ability to find stability through inner assurance, which can lead to an existence that does not require external control. The more we concentrate our gaze solely on solving the factual, the more we squander the potential within us.

The future of a humane medicine can only be to enable hope alongside plans and the desire for healing, because through hope suffering will not be eliminated, but its *totalising* nature can be beaten. Hope can helpstop suffering taking over completely. In doing so, hope proves to be a point of access to our inner freedom, an opening to the future and allows us to trust in being able to overcome what seems futile. We need a medical practice that is based on relationships and conversations, which can help people who are ill not to despair of their illness. It must be able to support them in developing new confidence in their own resources. That is the most profound and comprehensive therapy which can be offered. In the future, we must do everything we can to ensure that every person can hope to receive such life supporting medical treatment.

We have now come a long way, from fate, learning to accept, being able to trust and to hope. It should be clear that no-one can be truly happy if no space is found for these three dispositions. However, this space does not appear by itself.

When we are confronted with existential questions, we need another person we can talk to and who understands how we feel. Without this feeling of knowing we are understood, particularly if we are ill, we will neither achieve self-affirmation nor experience trust or even be able to hope, since all these values are companionship and community based and cannot thrive in a solipsistic reflection on oneself. Thus, the central and final point of my thematic reflections is understanding as the main challenge for a truly interpersonal form of medical practice, which I am putting forward in this book as the answer to people experiencing distress from illness.

8. Understanding people who are ill

»At every juncture, understanding opens up a new world.«

Wilhelm Dilthey

In a study outpatients were asked what for them was the most important factor contributing to the success of their treatment. The answer chosen most often was: »Talking to someone who understands me.«[1] This result alone shows how essential it is that we first understand the person we wish to help. Today, understanding is becoming increasingly difficult because medicine as a natural science is choosing a path of knowledge which does not take into account the world the person lives in. When we consider scientificity to primarily concern measuring and objectifying, it implies that human beings also have to be understood through generalisable and verifiable explanatory principles. We believe we can interpret people in the same way we interpret results and look for regularities, verifiable fixed criteria, and generalisations. As was shown in the introductory chapter, science views a sick person as a model for an illness, so to speak, whilst the sick person disappears behind that model. Within the context of medical practice shaped by science and economics, a person who is not a model, but rather a distinctive

---

[1] P. M. Murphy, D. Cramer a. F. J. Lillie, »The relationship between curative factors perceived by patients in their psychotherapy and treatment outcome: An exploratory study«. In: *British Journal of Medical Psychology* 57 (1984), pp. 187–192.

and unique individual, must therefore feel fundamentally misunderstood.

In saying this, I am in no way questioning the legitimacy of a scientific approach to the human being, on the contrary. In many cases, in the last two hundred years, it has proved to be beneficial. However, it is not enough. Human individuals with their very own particular biography can indeed be better classified (in the sense of the specific elaboration of a particular category) by the general laws of science, but the individuals themselves cannot be subsumed under them and they cannot be fully understood by them. The essence of humans as living beings cannot be described by their scientific properties, since in doing so we have understood nothing about them as a human being. This is the reason why understanding is so crucial.

The importance of understanding using schizophrenia as an example

Perhaps the best way to illustrate the importance of understanding is by way of an example. To do this, I have chosen the example of schizophrenia. A patient suffering from this psychosis once commented in a self-awareness report: »I often have the feeling that people who are ill cannot explain and people who are healthy cannot understand.«[2] There are so many patients who despair, not on account of their symptoms, but simply because no-one understands them. People

[2] Katrin Nehring, »Pflege bei Schizophrenie und wahnhaften Störungen«. in: M. Gassmann, W. Marschall, J. Utschakowski (Eds.), *Psychiatrische Gesundheits- und Krankenpflege.* (Heidelberg: Springer 2006), pp. 263–269, here p. 265.

with psychotic disorders, in particular, suffer from a medical process of treatment that tends to undervalue the importance of understanding. From a patient's perspective, doctors frequently appear to only be interested in them as carriers of symptoms and not as people. Modern medical practice focuses entirely on finding and treating symptoms, whereas a sick person's perspective is a different one. Patients suffering from a psychosis do not primarily perceive symptoms, but rather find themselves subjected to a world they find hostile and alien, and to a life thrown of course by illness. Their basic state is the feeling of being alienated. Such a feeling cannot simply be treated with medication, as important and indispensable as these might be. We can only really help sick people when we understand their experience of the illness and their existential crisis. Treating people who have schizophrenia means first and foremost treating their suffering alongside their symptoms, and to do this we have to understand how and what they are suffering from. We will only know how to help them when we have understood this suffering. The suffering of people with schizophrenia, in most cases these are young people, is primarily social suffering. Suffering from lost prospects, the reactions of others and the stigma of the illness. The lives of these people have been torn apart by the illness and they are constantly faced with a new life of social disintegration. Above all the illness has caused even those closest to them to perceive them, the mentally ill, in a different way.

Medical practice concentrates on the symptoms of schizophrenia and patients suffer from these as well: they suffer from acute symptoms, with their extreme anxiety, and they suffer primarily from the negative symptoms of associated avolition. These symptoms can be treated with medication; and it is the medication which can minimise the frequency of the episodes of the illness and hence its stabilising and resulting socialising function should not be underestimated. However, there is a form of suffering that remains, suffering caused by the loss of the feeling of self-worth. The psychiatrist Asmus Finzen expresses this suffering aptly: »People with schizophrenia suffer from the awareness that they no longer fit the image of the person they were because they sense that close friends and family do not value them, but instead the person they used to be.«[3]

When we consider this experience seriously, it becomes clear what therapy must entail. It should essentially free patients from their isolation and give them the assurance that they are people who are valued, now, *in* their illness, and not just in their condition before the illness. However, in order to communicate this appreciation, one thing is indispensable and that is understanding. Without understanding, this communication will not succeed, for the sick people will not be able to experience this feeling of self-worth if they do not feel understood. It is precisely this value of the feeling of being understood which the above-mentioned study confirms.

If being understood is the main desire of a patient, then it is necessary to examine more closely what this understanding can mean. What is understanding? What is necessary in order to understand people who are ill? What does it really mean to understand another person, as a partner in dialogue, a counterpart, as a doctor, as a therapist and as a professional auxiliary?

---

[3] Asmus Finzen, *Schizophrenie. Die Krankheit verstehen, behandeln, bewältigen*. (Bonn: Psychiatrie-Verlag 2003).

Understanding means seeing the other person

One of the major impediments to the process of understanding is the idea that it is possible to *completely* understand another person. However, as human beings, we will never be capable of completely understanding other human beings, for the simple reason that they are someone else. So we must continually acknowledge that the other person remains another person and thus will always be mysterious, surprising and unpredictable. What can optimally be achieved in the understanding process is »gaining trust at a distance« (Helmuth Plessner), but never total deciphering. We will only do justice to another person when we free ourselves from the idea of a totalisation of understanding, for every claim we lay to total understanding raises the danger of monopolising the other person. Nietzsche was keenly aware of this: »To be understood? You do know what that means? – Comprendre c'est égaler.«[4] By desiring complete understanding, the danger of brushing over differences becomes virulent; in this case, we tend to negate the otherness and subsume the other person under a category we already know. Jochen Hörisch talks about the »rage of understanding«[5], which attempts to override every difference and every otherness in order to »level out« the other person, so to speak, and be able to classify him or her into existing categories.

Against this background, it is important to bear in mind that people do not just live *in* the world but also *interact* with it and thus are in a fundamentally open relationship with the world and with themselves. The actions and feelings of a per-

---

[4] Friedrich Nietzsche, »Nachgelassene Fragmente 1885–1887«. In: *Kritische Studienausgabe,* eds. by Giorgio Colli and Mazzino Montinari, vol. 12. (Munich: dtv and Berlin: De Gruyter 1999), p. 51.

[5] Jochen Hörisch, *Die Wut des Verstehens.* (Frankfurt am Main: Suhrkamp 1998).

son can never be traced back linearly to a particular phenomenon in the world, but are always the result of a complex mélange of previous experiences and of individual, or singular cognitive processing. Consequently, understanding initially demands nothing less than humility: humility in the face of a fundamental human unfathomableness. For a human being is not just simply a puzzle to be solved, as human beings always remain a mystery that can never be completely unravelled. Acknowledging this is important in order to guard against premature compartmentalisation; it is important to beware of objectifying the people we would like to understand and allowing their individuality to disappear through generalisation. Only basic dispositions, such as modesty and restraint, can prevent classifying others into preconceived ideas. It could be said that understanding has more to do with restrained circumspection than with assertive action.

The danger of categorically not-understanding patients is particularly high in modern medicine. Aspiring doctors become socially accustomed to not only delivering causal explanations for physical manifestations, but also for feelings. People who are ill are then subjected to explanations that have very little to do with them as living beings. Marie Ebner-Eschenbach illustrates the difference between causal explanation and genuine understanding when she writes: »People who only understand what can be explained understand little.« This can mean only one thing; that understanding means the particular and singular in the overall context and not something conforming to law, or something categorical. In order to understand other people, we have to first set aside wishing for linear and causal explanations and avoid classification. We cannot simply look for what is typically causal and act as if understanding is the unravelling of logical argumentation, but rather we must free ourselves from causal analytic thinking and turn towards what makes a person unique;

which implies orienting ourselves towards a concrete situation, towards a singularity. This shift towards distinctiveness does not require a logical, but rather (in the Kantian sense) an »aesthetic« judgment, since the particular can only be deduced from the whole and not simply derivated from it. In brief, in the process of understanding we are not dealing with formal derivations, but rather with the willingness to react to the distinctive history of the other person, and that can only be successful if we recognise the otherness of the other person. For medical practice, this means we can only understand patients when we realise that, in our encounter with them, we are going beyond what is self-evident and are dealing with a unique individual. Medical practice finds it difficult to go beyond what is self-evident because it is socially obliged to think in categories. Often the diagnosis intervenes in the relationship between doctor and patient, which prevents all understanding, because it suggests that there is nothing left to understand above and beyond the diagnosis. Recognising the diagnosis, whilst at the same time leaving it behind, that is the art of understanding in medical treatment.

Trying to understand from a distance

Understanding is something very challenging, for, on the one hand, it calls for us to let someone in and on the other hand it requires distance. If we identify completely with the someone else and make their feelings our own, we may indeed feel a lot, but have we really understood? Understanding requires closeness and distance at the same time, for although closeness alone does imply reflection, it does not imply understanding. Detachment is also necessary in order to understand others, because the critical-analytical moment, which is a prerequisite for understanding, can only play a part at a distance. The more I identify myself inwardly with other people, the more I run the risk of seeing myself in them and not really seeing them in their own way. What it comes down to is that I put aside my own feelings because I have to recognise that the feelings which I have are inevitably oriented towards me. In order to really be with the other person, I must overcome this orientation towards myself and be in a position to give my feelings up to understanding. Thus, it is about trying to understand at a distance, which is in the second instance connected with feelings, but first and foremost with recognition. The philosopher Heidemarie Bennent-Vahle describes the virtue necessary for this as »reflective open-mindedness«,[6] which can also be expressed as »comprehending«: a cognitive activity which is primarily dependent on a reflective power of judgment, which can *also* refer back to intuition, but which is never completed by it.

If understanding relates to a reflective power of judgment, then we also recognise its ability to be taught. To that effect, understanding is »teachable«, in that it refers to the fundamental relevance of this reflective power of judgment. It teaches future doctors how they can, with this judgment, achieve a synthesis that makes it easier for them to integrate the patient's biography, the course of the illness and the patient's experience with suffering into the patient's general description in such a way that these elements become more understandable. I can only truly understand the feelings of someone else when I locate them in their biography and retell them, so to speak, from the beginning. In this way, understanding proves to be a case of connecting two levels, the level of intersubjectivity and the level of observation. When we

---

[6] Heidemarie Bennent-Vahle, *Mit Gefühl denken. Einblicke in die Philosophie der Emotionen.* (Freiburg/Munich: Verlag Karl Alber 2013), p. 207.

want to understand we must both immerse ourselves and maintain an overview. We must be both *with* the other person as well as an impartial observer. This is precisely what makes understanding so demanding. In any case, understanding is more than an emotional immersion because it forces us to widen our perspectives. And this brings me to the next point.

Placing specifics in the context of the whole

Understanding can always only begin when we simultaneously begin to take the feelings of the other person seriously. »To take them seriously« means perceiving and appreciating these feelings in the way they were expressed, but at the same time recognising their seriousness and meaning for the other person. Hence, understanding always implies the ability to step back from the here and now, to recognise that the other person's feelings are related to the present moment, and to wish to see the whole picture. We can be »hopelessly« caught up in the here and now, and understanding signifies trying to overcome being caught up by getting involved in a reconstructive and analytical way in what is being experienced. This is both a very demanding and sensitive process, but at the same time unavoidable: we have to know the patients' history in order to truly understand their feelings at the present moment. In this respect, understanding has always something to do with grasping the meaning of something, the meaning of something which can only result from the (maximum possible) scope of the patient's history. Understanding people who are ill or suffering means understanding their history. Only when we have taken into account, or better still, internalised, this history, will it be possible to look carefully at the particular perspective of the patients and at the same time widen their present »hopelessly« narrowing point of view. Admittedly, there is a very fine line between opening up new perspectives and patronising. And yet without this risk, understanding cannot succeed in breaking open what is present, specific and close by, for only by doing this can the whole play its part. Understanding does not mean just simply reflecting, but rather embedding ideas in a context, occasionally also correcting or introducing new perspectives and enabling different points of view. So understanding has always something to do with a cautious approach to the patient and less to do with disclosure. It involves a steady approach to the patient, which is essentially never complete.

Understanding people who are ill is a great challenge for medical practice, because it does not constitute a scientific methodology, but instead is interpersonal. It is not about discovering objective connections that inalterably apply and can be ascertained or even proven. Many people believe implicitly that, if handled in the right way, they can have a ready explanation for all phenomena of human existence. And yet ultimately, such thinking is based on a categorical mistake. This desire for a full explanation can indeed be fulfilled with regard to objects and machines, but not in relation to people. A person does not live in a closed, causally determined system, but instead, as mentioned above, lives as a free being in constant interaction with the world, and, due to this freedom, continually changes and the world in which the person lives.

It is necessary to underline and emphasise the one-sidedness of a causal and mechanistic approach to medical treatment, which has become socially acceptable again in the combination of science and economy, and which inevitably goes hand in hand with a levelling of the uniqueness of human beings. For if, as happens by implication these days, we were to take a person to be a causally determined mechanism, who must be dealt with as quickly as possible, this would ultimately result in us not having to »understand« any more, as the correct treatment would already be decided by the objective facts. As much as our health system adheres to this concept, we must be adamant that, without understanding, we are faced with a »hopeless« situation, where no-one can be truly helped. Understanding in the true sense of the word is not speedy understanding, nor a causal, logical search for causes, but is understanding that works step by step, understanding which is not geared towards establishing unambiguity, but rather accepting ambiguity as an everyday reality. There is no right or wrong here. What is needed is a coherent outline of the situation. If we want to understand we do not want to understand as we usually would. We would like to focus on what is unique, to understand anew, and understanding anew does not mean ascribing things, but rather withstanding a certain limbo: it may be one thing or another. It may be what I already know or even something new, which I first have to comprehend.

Understanding means exposing oneself

Understanding cannot be achieved from outside and it cannot be interpreted as the result of a purely observational relationship, for we can only understand by immersing ourselves in the process and by getting involved and familiarising ourselves with the other person. People can put *themselves* in someone else's position, this is how our language puts it. The language is very explicit here; it does not say that someone can simply detect something in another person, but rather it says that they must expose *themselves* to a situation in order to truly understand. This indicates that the process of understanding is not possible without involving oneself. As Wilhelm Schapp says, we are inextricably »entangled in histories«[7], and therefore do not only begin to understand when we explicitly interpret the world, but understand, as Martin Heidegger points out, solely by having been put into this world. People »always« bring a pre-understanding with them which originates from their own world. However, people who understand do not simply stand still in the development of their understanding, but try to also take others' pre-understanding seriously and by doing so become conscious of the contingency of their own pre-understanding. This is precisely the meaning of the concept of exposing *oneself*. The people who are truly able to understand are the ones capable of exposing themselves to dialogue to such an extent that the other person's view becomes equally as valuable as their own and can therefore resonate with their own view of things. A true dialogical experience is an experience of our own bias and thus at the same time disposes us to widen our horizons. In the process of understanding we realise that we could think differently, feel differently and be different to the way we are. Hans-Georg Gadamer illustrated this beautifully: Real understanding is nothing more than the coalescence of two horizons. Learning to understand involves a mutual approach to each other, an approximation of both horizons, which combine to form a new perspective. Yet this can only succeed if I allow myself to get involved in this unfamiliar horizon of understanding. Whoever takes understanding seriously will have to be prepared to allow themselves to be instructed by the other person, to allow themselves to be carried off into that person's world to the extent that, in a sense,

[7] Wilhelm Schapp, *In Geschichten verstrickt. Zum Sein von Mensch und Ding*. (Wiesbaden: B. Heymann 1976 [1953]).

they are enhanced and changed by taking this world seriously.

Understanding is not merely a result, but instead is subject to preconditions whose central feature is that, when understanding, we fundamentally »understand each other mutually«. This fundamental attitude towards mutual understanding does not, of course, mean considering everything that the other person says or does to be good. Rather, it means that we take the other person in their world seriously and assume that what they say and do is reasonable, indeed speaks to us. The word understanding, therefore, does not only imply an intellectual achievement but also a character virtue: a disposition of goodwill or benevolence. We enter into the process of understanding freely and with a disposition of goodwill, which essentially means that understanding is always accompanied by a sense of agreement.

In the light of this it has become clear that understanding involves more than empathising with someone: what we wish to understand cannot be brought to bear through the capacity to empathise, nor through a mere recapitulation of what the other person says. When we understand, we take part in something neither we nor others simply have within us. Understanding is a process of sharing, of being a part of, of taking a share, and so a process of developing things in common. Ultimately, understanding means sharing a sense of meaning. It manifests itself as common ground, which lies, so to speak, in the »between«. Gadamer calls it the dialogue which gives rise to understanding between two people, an understanding which does not simply double the view of one person or the other, but rather sets its sights on a mutually shared experience. An experience which does not stem from the other person, but from the actual dialogue, and thus does not simply come about through reflection, but by speaking to the other person.

Understanding means spending time

Understanding is, therefore, a process that must develop step by step and cannot be seen as the logical result of a directive, a procedure or a method, but rather should be understood as an occurrence beyond the control of our planning. Although understanding is reliant on presuppositions and conditions, it is not just about the result of these conditions, but rather represents what is fundamentally new and evolves from these conditions. Understanding is an »emergence«. Something which cannot be managed, but appears, rises up and takes shape. There is no such thing as »managing understanding«, but instead a successful management of those conditions which allow understanding to evolve.

In other words, we do not understand other people because we actively make an effort to do so, but rather because we are receptive. We have to give the process of understanding space in order to allow an atmosphere of calm, confidence, circumspection, freedom from pressure and guaranteed success. Understanding has something to do with allowing for time; it cannot be forced or pushed into action, but rather only allowed to develop with the other person at a calm, leisurely pace.

We cannot plan to understand, but we can try to get involved to such an extent that we ultimately take part in a process of understanding that leads us to new ideas, new insights and new horizons. People who understand not only recognise something they already know, they continually open up to something new and set out on paths which go in unknown directions. It is precisely because understanding is not a discovery or an experience but rather an opening up to things, a design and thus a creative practice, that we can talk about the »art of understanding«. Something new is created, whose special feature is that it cannot simply be manufactured, but instead can only be developed in a creative process. The core of this development lies in the internal attitude adopted. Genuine understanding is only possible through inner composure, patience and tolerance, as it enables those who are helping not to categorise others according to prearranged theories, but experience them as individuals. This quote from André Gide expresses it well: »Ce n'est pas du tout qu'elle soit incapable de comprendre, mais elle veut trop vite avoir compris.«[8] An integral part of understanding is patience, for only when we are patient can we succeed in not pressurising others into a prefabricated model of explanation and interpretation, which does not do justice to its uniqueness.

Understanding means recognising direction

We are told in both medicine and psychology that it is essentially about analysing, dissecting and establishing causal relationships. All of this is, of course, necessary, for we can only know the direction the treatment will take when we are conscious of where something comes from. However, by looking at where something comes from, the crucial part of the treatment is not touched upon. If we only concerned ourselves with where the illness had come from, we would limit our understanding of the person in need of help and possibly want to take them back to their situation before the origin of the illness. This does not do justice to life, which always strives forwards. Consciousness of where something has come from is in fact only a thin crutch in comparison to the consciousness of the possibility of where we can go to. In the end, the possibility of where to is more important than ana-

---

[8] André Gide, Journal 1889–1939. 14th January 1912, cited in Hans Robert Jauß: *Wege des Verstehens.* (Munich: Fink 1994), p. 51.

lysing where from, since simply viewing their possibilities can help people under pressure to take their life in hand, gain more security and develop new perspectives.

Understanding people who are ill means, first and foremost, recognising their potential within their acute suffering, sensing the glimmer of an awakening within their acute lethargy, and seeing their struggle to escape, their longing for new horizons in their current feeling of being trapped in thoughts of loss. Peter F. Schmid, a psychotherapist and theologian, compares a therapist to a gardener, who »has no direct influence on the appearance of the plant, but certainly on what can become of the plant in accordance with its inherent possibilities.«[9] I find this image very apposite, as it shows that healing, namely the mastering of the crisis, is not ultimately within the helper's power, and yet the helper can ensure that it happens, through the patients themselves. In order for this to happen, the helper must exercise care and concern, and a key part of this concern is creating an atmosphere where the patient is given space to grow. Understanding is like humus on which the personality of the person seeking help can grow.

Conclusions for medical practice

What conclusions can be drawn for modern medical practice? It has become clear that the treatment of people needing help can only be successful if it can be seen as a dialogue of understanding, for only in the form of a dialogue can people who are suffering find the recognition that they are understood

[9] Peter F. Schmid, *Personale Begegnung. Der personzentrierte Ansatz in Psychotherapie, Beratung, Gruppenarbeit und Seelsorge.* (Würzburg: Echter 1995), p. 102.

and have the feeling of being taken seriously. Along with this insight, we have to recognise that simple expressions such as »speaking more«, »more time« and »words are valuable« are not enough, for they do not really tackle the basic problem. Yes, there is not enough time for conversation, yes, conversation is not paid adequately, yes, more peace and quiet for conversation would be a great help and yet all of this would not solve the current crisis. For it is not *primarily* time, money or structure which is lacking most. It is the inner attitude towards the spoken word and the attitude towards the person who is suffering which are missing. It is only this attitude which turns the answer into an answer. Even if this attitude is deformed by incentivising schemes, by training over-focused on one area and misguided socialisation, it cannot simply be cured by changing external circumstances. It can only become established when we realise how crucial care is in any form of treatment.

We could ask: is it enough to simply understand another person? Is that not too little? As a person in need of help would we not be more likely to look for a person who solves the problem rather than one who analyses it? Understanding cannot be everything, for understanding alone does not change the frequently painful reality of a person who is seeking help. Understanding cannot simply turn adverse experience into something positive. The experience must be recognised as something against which understanding is certainly powerless. However, understanding can decisively shape the relationship between people in need of help and their unfavourable reality. It is important that an indication of the possibilities ensues, that in understanding, a general overview can be gained and experience can be looked back on. The main thrust of my considerations on understanding is by no means arguing that medical practice can be complete solely through understanding. Rather, my considerations must be viewed as pointers to the fact that by our ubiquitous devaluation of understanding and our one-sided focus on what is objectifiable, we are not fulfilling the actual task of medical practice. And we run the danger of not only leaving the patient alone but are ultimately not able to help him in spite of the procedures. Essentially, the core meaning of understanding can only be explained anthropologically, for the human desire to be understood by others is ultimately based on the even deeper longing to overcome the feeling of alienation from the world.[10] That is also the underlying reason for the curative power of understanding. Along with the experience of being understood by another person goes the experience of no longer feeling alienated in a hostile world, but instead knowing that one is comfortable and safe with one's own feelings. Rooted in every person is a deep desire, which can be understood as a longing to feel familiar with the world and to feel at home within it. Illness can shatter this feeling and, as we have seen in several examples, can dramatically highlight a person's loneliness. The feeling of profound loneliness, when confronted with an unexpected illness, and the suffering caused by the experience of loneliness and alienation, constitute the horror of illness, and this suffering can only be offset and alleviated through an understanding person. If we are dealing with the body, but simply push this feeling to one side, we leave the sick alone in their suffering and this only reaffirms the loneliness that has been brought on by the illness. An understanding partner can enable an experience of companionship and thus make someone aware that they are not living in an antagonistic world and at the same time can make clear to them that they do not have to overcome the great challenge of their illness alone.

---

[10] Emil Angehrn, *Sinn und Nicht-Sinn. Das Verstehen des Menschen.* (Tübingen: Mohr-Siebeck 2011), p. 29f.

IV.
Caring is everything

»Wherever there is genuine conversation, there is therapy.«

Walter von Baeyer

On the previous pages, we learnt of the existential challenges of different illnesses and crisis situations and used the concepts of acceptance, trust, hope and understanding to explore core subjects, which can be helpful in overcoming these existential experiences. The starting point was the reference to the type of medical practice which is often speechless and helpless in regard to these experiences. Modern medicine, which, as previously described, is essentially industrially oriented, runs counter to its own purpose, as it increasingly seems to forget that ultimately every treatment occurs in an encounter between people, which is unique and defies standardisation.

Encounters as the basis for healing

Our work on understanding in the last section identified a basic issue: it is not just about technical procedures or the application of a particular method, but rather primarily what kind of relationship there is to the patient when the treatment is carried out. This relationship has less to do with a particular action and more to do with an attitude. Essentially, healing can be understood to be the result of an encounter, a coming together; it cannot be understood simply to be the product of an application. Why is this the case? What is an encounter all about in the context of medical practice? I would like to mention three aspects which I consider important for the process of treatment.

Every encounter is initially linked to limitations of time

and place: people cannot encounter each other constantly and everywhere, but only when someone comes from somewhere and will move on to somewhere else. This means that encounters are inherently and invariably transitory, and are not intended to last over a longer period of time. This is particularly true of encounters between a doctor and a patient. Patients come from somewhere and will continue on their path, and for a certain time we form a bond with them. Yet we all know the feeling of meeting someone, talking to him or her, and then afterwards realising that we did not really meet them at all. What is the reason for this? An encounter happens when the other person, at the very moment we become aware of him or her, actually becomes present to us, which interrupts the familiar und typical course of things. The word encounter evokes the idea of pausing for a moment; it suspends the habitual and allows the flow of routine to stop for a moment. It is not primarily other people's call for help which makes me pause; initially it is their simple suggestion of »here I am« that attracts my attention. It is only in taking the second step that I react to their call, react to their expectation, to their request.

Drawing on Emmanuel Levinas's idea, we might say that the strongest and most basic request can be seen in the »countenance« of other people, in their presence, which emanates wordlessly from their being and which »speaks« to me in our encounter. Encountering other people means being spoken to by their presence. This explains why we meet some individuals, speak to them, continue on our way and yet have not actually encountered them: we merely perceived other people's presence, but were not really aware of their being.

Overcoming instrumental rationality

The Jewish religious philosopher Martin Buber writes in his book *The Dialogic Principle*: »All means are an obstacle. Only when all means have been left aside, does an encounter ensue.«[1] Buber emphasises that the characteristic feature of an encounter is that we leave the immediate purposes behind and »move« entirely towards the person. In an encounter, functionality, goal, and instrumental access take second place to the person. Michael Theunissen rightly points out that »means« here can also be understood to have a second meaning, namely in the sense of a »medium« (as pre-concepts, abstract concepts, intentions or agreed targets) by means of which other people appear to us and by means of which we all too easily define them.[2] Roman Guardini has a similar view when he describes people in an encounter as follows: »Their being shows itself and requires, beyond all other functions, that it be seen and valued in itself.«[3]

But is it at all useful, in the context of medical practice and therapy, to talk of an encounter? Does the field of medicine itself not pursue a purpose and is, therefore, instrumental *per se*? Therapists want to fulfil the purpose of helping, healing and relieving. In this sense, their encounter with the person who is suffering is anything but a purpose free environment. Yet the concept of an encounter does contain something which is especially important for medical practice. It clearly illustrates that, ultimately, the aim of helping can only be achieved when we address the whole person. For as

---

[1] Martin Buber, *Das dialogische Prinzip.* (Heidelberg: L. Schneider 1965), p. 15.
[2] Michael Theunissen, *Der Andere. Studien zur Sozialontologie der Gegenwart.* (Berlin: De Gruyter 1977), p. 263.
[3] Romano Guardini, *Welt und Person.* (Würzburg: Werkbund 1950), p. 127.

long as we only look for ways to cure the patients' symptoms, we are viewing them as an object which can be skilfully »tampered with«. It is only in an encounter that the person emerges from behind the object, theory and standard concept. Following on from Martin Buber, Carl Rogers, the psychologist and psychotherapist, has shown that the real »champions« of healing, alleviation and overcoming are not the therapists, but the people who are suffering, and the more we make *them* the focal point and allow them to have their say, without placing them in an instrumental relationship, the more we enable them to reflect on their own potential. It could also be expressed as follows: in a genuine encounter with a person seeking help, the suggestion of wanting to help increasingly dissipates and is replaced by the increasing desire to experience *who* the other person is. The question of means or methods of helping are secondary to the question of the being of the other, the cosmos of their own personality within their own world.

Recognition

In a genuine encounter I, therefore, acknowledge other people in their whole personal existence. This recognition prohibits the appropriation of their person, overpowering them and subsuming them under a specified pattern, as this would destroy the personal quality of the relationship to the other person. This is why the concept of encounter is essential in treatment; it demonstrates how important it is to get away from the idea of wanting to teach something to the person looking for help. This teaching already assumes a predefined concept. Genuine change, however, cannot be predefined, it must be brought about by other people according to their own ideas and aims. Only when we try to open up to other people in a dialogical process will it be possible to awaken self-realisation tendencies within them.

When treating people in need of help, it is simply not enough to offer them a technical procedure or promote the latest treatment methods. Help is not a consumer product and not a finished product to be bought. Concrete support is something that has to be extracted little by little in a dialogue. For only when the people helping get involved in the life of the person seeking help, when they open themselves up to and are guided by the unique nature of the other person, will the common path they can take become clear. Without an encounter with the patient, there would be no indication as to which intervention, which method and which procedure should be adopted, as the indications of a procedure do not simply result from the objective facts, but rather from the connection between these objective facts and the specific history of the patient. No indication is possible without an encounter; without it the choice of further treatment procedures would ultimately be purely arbitrary or correspond to the preference of the therapist, but would certainly not be the adequate solution to the specific situation the person who is suffering is in. Every reflective doctor or therapist knows that an encounter with a patient always represents a fresh confrontation with a person who did not previously exist for the helper; either in consultation or even in their textbooks and published studies: every patient is an individual and requires a unique answer, which can only be given when health care professionals knows *who* is sitting opposite them.

Encountering the person who is sick lies at the centre of treatment, not least because real care can only be given within an encounter. For we can only talk about care when it addresses a specific person and not a standardised »case«. Martin Buber expresses this aptly when he writes that every encounter has »a new face«. An encounter is, therefore, always an encounter with a particular person in a particular situation, and this situational nature of an encounter inevitably involves a demand made by the other person in the encounter. We owe the other person an answer. Werner Faber rightly speaks of the »demanding nature of an encounter«,[4] since it demands from us an answer, which is both appropriate to the situation and is a committed and personal assumption of responsibility, not a casual or noncommittal reaction. In an encounter of this type, care signifies confronting another person as a person and feeling called upon to be interested in them and to support them in an authentic way. Consequently, it serves much more than the mere function of preparing further stages of treatment tailored to the patient. Healing power evolves from caring, which is important to focus on, as it is significantly underestimated by our current health system. What is this healing power of care which therefore supports treatment?

Caring enhances

Care rescues other people from anonymity, turns them into someone special and allows them to be seen in a new light. Not in the first instance, by us, but rather *they see themselves* in a new light. It ennobles them and in so doing provides an antidote to the severe danger of sick people stereotyping themselves. It does not belittle them, but builds them up and in this manner has the potential to develop their per-

[4] Werner Faber, »Zum Problem der Begegnung. Anthropologische und pädagogische Anmerkungen«. In: Ibid. (Ed.), *Pädagogische Kontroversen*. Volume 1. (Munich: Fink 1969), pp. 123–138, here p. 129.

sonality. Simply by caring we show that they can be who they are, they learn to accept themselves (as people who are ill). An encounter and caring understanding represent a profound form of esteem, which changes the patient. To put it another way: our relationship to them influences their relationship to themselves. For people in need almost always find themselves in a demoralised state, where they have lost their basic trust in the world and in themselves. In this stressful situation, care can be an antidote, a »remedy«, because it restores this very ability.

However, care not only entails reassurance and trust in the world around us. The feeling of being accepted and heard pushes us to a deeper level of consciousness, where we dare to question our past, often for the first time. Every genuine dialogue brings about change and realignment, because we gradually escape from our own repression mechanisms and want to play a role, to present and reposition ourselves. The assurance granted us by care, to be able to be who we are, controls our fear and allows us to question superficialities. The other person encourages us to also take a critical look at ourselves, as knowing that someone is listening to us, encourages us to listen to ourselves.

Caring transforms

Gabriel Marcel has described understanding and care as a blessing from which »a mysterious impulse to creation«[5] emanates. He expresses the crucial effect of care: that a person can be empowered by an understanding partner not to be

---

[5] Gabriel Marcel, *Das ontologische Geheimnis.* (Stuttgart: Reclam 1961), p. 44.

content with unfavourable circumstances, but instead to transform them creatively. This is what is meant by creative power. It becomes apparent at the moment when the people needing help become conscious that what is within them cannot simply be »revealed« and calculated (and conversely cannot be denied to them!), but rather lies dormant in them, as an inviolable source of development, which Marcel rightly describes as a »mystery«. It is a mystery, because we can never know in advance which potential coping strategies we can uncover from deep within us. The interpersonal relationship which is realised in caring can pave the way to this potential because the dialogue with the other person raises awareness and deepens experience. An interpersonal relationship has the effect of deepening our experience and offers us the opportunity to attain a level that remains closed to us as individuals trapped in the here and now.

In conversation with patients it is important to make it clear that they are essentially seeking to understand themselves, owing to the fact that they have become alienated through their illness or other adverse experiences. On this path to self-awareness we need another person to share this desire for understanding with us. For the desire to understand oneself cannot be satisfied without talking to someone. All of us are innately endowed with a natural power to develop and grow. However, this can only fully blossom when we come into contact with other people, through whom we can get to know ourselves and experience ourselves. The other person represents the necessary condition for developing this dormant power further. Only in this way can we grasp the full significance of the importance of understanding and care.

The significance of conversation

At this point, it is important to return once more to understanding and conversation. Emmanuel Levinas wrote the following sentence, which encapsulates the importance of conversation: »Understanding a person already implies a true conversation.«[6] In saying this, Levinas is pointing out that the moment of speaking with the other poeple already implies that you wish to allow them to be themselves. Allowing someone to speak already signifies, in a sense, the acceptance of the otherness of other people, for otherwise one would be speaking at them. Allowing them to speak out means listening to them, leaving room for their own opinion, and respecting them as someone who has something to say to us. We can see why Hjördis Nerheim, the philosopher and care researcher, defines communication as follows: »Communication, in the strict sense, does not mean an exchange of language, but rather a broadening of perspectives in one's own life through contact with another person.«[7] Not only understanding, but also true communication transforms people.

We have to ask critically: does such a conversation in the true sense actually take place in modern medical practice? There is no doubt that we have to recognise that there is now a greater awareness for the need of conversation, and there are now related units in students' training courses. Yet far too often, conversation is reduced to conversational techniques based on instrumental rationality. Prospective doctors are, for instance, taught techniques for how they are to speak to achieve a good »outcome«, or which rhetorical methods

---

[6] Emmanuel Levinas, *Zwischen uns. Versuche über das Denken an den Anderen*. (Munich: Hanser, 1995), p. 17.

[7] Hjördis Nerheim, *Die Wissenschaftlichkeit der Pflege*. (Bern: Huber 2001), p. 201.

can signal empathy. Consequently, they are not taught how they can open themselves to the world of experience of the person who is ill, but instead how they can use emotion for the purposes of a successful treatment. Similar in style to the »customer pitch«, a new »culture of conversation« has been established, a culture of stage-managed conversations, which actually represents nothing more than a culture of inauthentic and strategic conversation. When people learn to use words, not in an understanding way, but purely strategically, they run the risk of allowing the conversation to degenerate into superficiality, even sometimes into a speech bubble. This has nothing to do with medical treatment based on relationships, or understanding, or indeed care.

Medical treatment based on spoken relationships can only be realised when we regard the word not as a function or an instrumental rational means, but rather as a »gift« which finds its expression primarily in connection with the other person. It makes an important difference whether we understand speaking in a medical context to be a strategy or in fact an expression of appreciation, an act of addressing someone, or a form of resonance. As important as strategy and information transfer may be, on their own they inhibit a relationship. It can only truly be a relationship when the word, beyond its intentional function, is taken to be a gift, with which we communicate to the people we are speaking to that they can speak directly to us and are fundamentally important to us.

The significance of listening

The spoken word is not enough. Listening is even more important than speaking. Arguably the weakest point in modern medical practice is that it not only devalues the importance of conversation, but much more seriously the importance of listening. We have »lost sight of« listening because visual perspectives are favoured in medical practice and auditory expressions are overlooked. Evidence is given only through »autopsy«, under the predominance of an ocular paradigm, i. e. through the visualisation of structure and material, but not through audible perception. This »optocentrism« (Lothar Quandt) makes a doctor susceptible to slipping purely into an observer's perspective and turning the patient into an object to be observed and reduced to reportable findings. This is a fundamental problem of modern medical practice. In this way, it distances itself further from the patient's actual world of experience, because it can only be heard, but cannot be optically represented. In other words: what the patient has, we can see, who he is, we can only hear.

Against this background, it is even more important not to associate understanding primarily with visual, documentable and verifiable speech, but instead more fundamentally with skilful listening. Our language is full of visual paradigms, and so we talk about »mental representation«, about envisioning, about internal images, but for true understanding, concepts such as awareness, introspection and resonance are more important. As a result of its scientific bias, modern medical practice gives preference to observation, documentation, illustration, verification and quantification, and neglects listening, for what is heard cannot easily be substantiated and utilised as »evidence«. The tendency to neglect listening is not only due to a scientific bias in medical practice, but also to economisation, in the sense that an obligation to account, verify and document has become a part of daily life in medical practice. Instead of resonance, we talk of »transparency« and »evidence«, which, for their part, are derived from the metaphor of light and the primacy of seeing rooted in this metaphor; even the words suggest, that there is nothing important to hear.

The quality of listening cannot be substantiated, and so it is disappearing ever more from modern medical practice, which sees itself as a quality controlled production facility. For unlike seeing, hearing is linked to a particular moment. We always hear in the here and now; what is heard cannot be »frozen in time« like an image. Thus it is unavoidably remains fleeting and ephemeral. Yet medical practice, which only sees and no longer hears, is becoming superficial, for hearing speaks to us much more profoundly than seeing. The reason for this is that it is much more closely associated with our corporeality. Hearing represents a particular form of incorporation; it absorbs the whole atmosphere, which resonates in the tone of voice and potentially says more in the silent pauses than in the actual spoken words. Let us remind ourselves: people suffering from dementia becomes ever more a hearing (resonating, listening) being, because their body becomes increasingly important, their self increasingly becomes a bodily self. If medical practice persists with its »optocentric« perspective, the dementia patient will simply become alienated and there will be no understanding. The primary importance of the visual in modern medical practice leads *à la longue* to the loss of »acroamatic« reason, which is energised by the ability to listen. Someone who only wants to see, will become blind without noticing it.

This loss of vision caused by only fixating on seeing is bound up with the fact that by following the visual paradigm, we primarily concentrate on something specific, something concrete. Anything that cannot be singled out in this way is overlooked. Seeing is always related to rendering visible, selecting and screening. We scan an area with our eyes and search out a point we want to observe in more detail. By contrast, when we hear we are not primarily targeting something particular and specific, but are open to what will present itself to us. With good reason, listening has also been described as »a sense of immersion« or »a sense for surroundings«.[8] The concept of immersion perfectly describes the idea that we always listen in on something whole. We do not understand the word as a distinctive construct, but rather we sense a mood, a tempo, a possible tremor or excitation in the voice, in other words the whole atmosphere which cannot be put into words and yet is inevitably present. As Johann Gottfried Herder puts it: »Whoever hears, hears a world«. The receptive and pathic moment of hearing opens us up to the indeterminate, unascertainable, to that which can be understood immediately during the process of hearing and is not something which must first be discriminated as something dot-like, in order to be grasped. When we listen to someone, we can only rarely determine the specific wording as something concrete, which is in turn to help us understand. Instead, we take in the whole of what we have heard over a period of time, with all its different sounds, and by means of this process, we have understood something which our eyes could never have conveyed. In the words of Erwin Strauss, the neurologist, psychologist and philosopher: »When we see, we capture the skeleton of things, when we listen, we capture their pulse.«[9] This once again points out how vital an open mode of listening is for genuine understanding.

Hearing is so crucial because, with our preference for the optical, we tend to see others from a distance. Seeing is a sense that entails distance and one that is egocentric. I can see or I can look away, I can see this or leave it in the back-

---

[8] Holger Schulze, »Hören des Hörens. Aporien und Utopien einer historischen Anthropologie des Klangs«. In: *Paragrana* 16 (2007) 2, pp. 240–244, here p. 244.

[9] Erwin Strauss, *Vom Sinn der Sinne. Ein Beitrag zur Grundlegung der Psychologie.* (Berlin: Springer 1956), p. 398.

ground, I can ignore something and it remains invisible. In short, I myself decide what I would like to see. Hearing is different: hearing is a mixture of activity and experiencing; when I am heard, I am understood; in a certain way I am vulnerably exposed when being heard. Above all, when I listen, I take a step back from myself because I orientate myself towards the other person. In the best possible sense, hearing is »listening to«; an intentional occurrence and at the same time involves exposing oneself. Hans Jonas describes it as an understanding »that something is happening that is beyond my control.«[10] Listening to someone, I step out of myself in such a way that I am with the other person and no longer only with myself. This makes listening something dialogical, perhaps even more so than speaking. For listening does not simply mean receiving a word; it represents the readiness to let what was spoken affect me. Heidegger expressed it in this way: »being able to listen does not first enable the relationship of the one person to the other, i. e. the companionship, but instead presupposes it.«[11]

Modern medical practice is increasingly lapsing into an atmosphere of drowning-out. It sells itself, it markets itself and becomes ever shriller and louder in extolling its methods. At the same time, it encourages the representatives of the medical profession to pursue the primacy of seeing, and is allowing listening to wither away and the patient to fall silent.[12] A medical practice which leads to both silence and deafness! This calamitous trend must be tackled with a new

---

[10] Hans Jonas, *Organismus und Freiheit. Ansätze zu einer philosophischen Biologie.* (Göttingen: Vandenhoeck & Ruprecht 1973), p. 202.

[11] Martin Heidegger, *Hölderlins Hymnen »Germanien« und »Der Rhein«*, ed. by Susanne Ziegler, GA, vol. 39, (Frankfurt am Main: Vittorio Klostermann 1999), p. 72.

[12] Barbara Duden, »Über Formen des Verstummens in der Begegnung des Patienten mit der Medizin«. In: *Intensiv erleben – Menschen in klinischen*

emphasis on listening and a new appreciation of hearing as an expression of genuine awareness.

Medical practice as the link between practicality and interpersonal relationship

Let us attempt a final overview with particular reference to specific inadequacies in modern medical practice. The current structural changes in modern medical practice are related to the key issue of whether the doctor-patient relationship is regarded as an interpersonal relationship or a competence-based service. Is the relationship between a person in need and a professional helper bound by unconditional care or by equivalence? Is it about benevolent dedication or dutiful compromise? A special feature of medical practice is perhaps that it can be both and perhaps even has to be. Every attempt at exclusion of one or the other could be accused of ideological thinking. This has simply to do with the fact that medical practice requires both the competence to justify action, which derives from rules and general knowledge, and at the same time demands a practical ability to decide, which is dependent on an interpretation of the particular situation in which the patients find themselves. Whilst the ability to justify refers back to subject knowledge, the ability to decide within a unique framework essentially only develops through hermeneutic knowledge. Therefore, medical practice is constantly caught between rules and particularity, between rote learning and improvising, between deducing from what is known and imaginative creation. The treatment of people who are ill is

---

Grenzsituationen, publ. by Tuğsal Moğul & Alfred Simon. (Berlin/Münster: LIT Verlag 2013), pp. 101–109.

an extremely challenging practice, which constantly requires an amalgamating synthesis in order to succeed.

Medical practice also occupies a special position, because, on the one hand, it takes place in a radically impersonal context: it is quantifiable and is an administrative act, which is documented and handed over to various authorities. It is both formal and formalised, as it acts on the basis of schemata, which are based on institutionally prescribed rules, practicality, objectivity and science. On the other hand, it has a deeply personal component: it thrives on interpersonal relationships, it is concerned with intimacy, demands affinity, emotional warmth and, above all else, empathetic understanding. To bring these two sides together represents a great challenge, which is not always met in everyday life, but which no-one can question as an ideal worth striving for.

The almost irresolvable ambivalence in this relationship lies in the area of tension between »formal« and »informal« and has to do with the basic desire to be treated as equals in a nevertheless structurally asymmetric relationship. This also includes the fusion of a personal desire to help and a professional occupation. In medical practice, an altruistic relationship geared towards helping, and a quantifiable relationship of service, collide with each other and this tension ultimately makes the relationship susceptible to swinging in one direction or the other.

However, the reason for the biggest area of tension is that it will not succeed without personal affinity and yet cannot be realised on a purely personal level. The relationship between a doctor and a patient is not a purely personal relationship, since, unlike friendship for example, it is not based on genuine mutuality. As soon as doctors starts asking patients for advice about their own problems, they stop being a doctor. It is also not a purely personal relationship because it is usually a temporary relationship and must be viewed as a socially established practice. Yet, a doctor-patient relationship without empathy and emotional warmth, which are characteristic features of private relationships, would not succeed. Doctors are essentially required to perform a dual role in therapeutic relationships. On the one hand, they need to be professional helpers and skilled experts, whilst on the other hand they will not be able to fulfil their role properly if they do not also see themselves as human beings in the encounter with the patient. Treating people who are ill implies a combination of procedures, the analytical use of understanding and a creative use of the »heart«. This is why a doctor's task is such a great challenge.

Against this background, a polarisation between procedures and relationships does not take the matter forward. When treating patients, it is not a question of »either/or«, but instead, of the right balance, of a complementary relationship. Procedure is indispensable, but it needs a relationship in order to be truly effective. Thus, a relationship does not represent a substitute for procedure, but rather a precondition for success. The more trustworthy, the more understanding and the more empathetic a doctor is seen to be, the greater effect the technical procedures will have. This is not only true of medical engineering, medication or medical intervention, but equally of conversational techniques, therapy techniques and analysis techniques. These specifically psychotherapeutic »techniques« will remain hopeless manoeuvres if therapists do not succeed in building up relationships to their patients, based on trust and warmth.

We can do our utmost to investigate, direct and treat a patient and yet all these approaches will be ineffectual if they are not accompanied by care and concern. For all these tasks cannot convey what understanding actually is: the reassurance that the person is valuable and worth concerning ourselves with. The overemphasis on action is often a desperate attempt to convey this message; however, if the action is not embedded in an understanding relationship, this mediation will be unsuccessful. This is the real reason for the indispensability of an understanding care. Only in this way will it be adequately emphasised to the people seeking help that they are important to us and that what they feel and think will not be brushed aside, but instead recognised as meaningful. Perhaps it is, ultimately, more important to know *who* the people are who have an illness than being able to categorise the illness they are suffering from. This is precisely the conclusion we are in a position to draw from the examples we have detailed in this book. Whether patients are suffering with chronic pain, whether they have cancer or the onset of dementia, they are always challenged to learn how to deal with these phenomena. This challenge allows them to discover new horizons for themselves and not feel at the mercy of their illness, despite its associated limitations. Along with the industrialisation and economisation of medical practice, we have completely lost sight of the necessity for an approach and attitude based on support. By supporting, we acknowledge people who are ill, and this allows them to discover a feeling of curative self-esteem within themselves. This is the real »key effect« of medical practice based on care.

Medical practice based on care, this is the appeal I have made in writing this book. It is an appeal for something which is no longer taken for granted in our streamlined health system, but which has to be re-evaluated as the core of medical, psychotherapeutic and nursing practice. At the present time, modern medical practice is structured in such a way that it seems more concerned with the treatment of healthy people than with sick people, who are dependent, in need of help, and often even in a state of despair. For it neglects to take into account an interpersonal connection with the people who are suffering which can support them, give them security and stabilise them again; not through constant support, but rather by mobilising their inner strengths. Caring elicits strength, it stimulates and awakens undreamt potential to overcome circumstances. It is, therefore, completely irresponsible to wish to tacitly make this very strength redundant through rationalisation. For in this case, medical practice is economising at the very core of its identity and this does not augur well for the future.

Name Index